MPLS and Label Switching Networks

ISBN 0-13-015823-2

Prentice Hall Series In
Advanced Communications Technologies

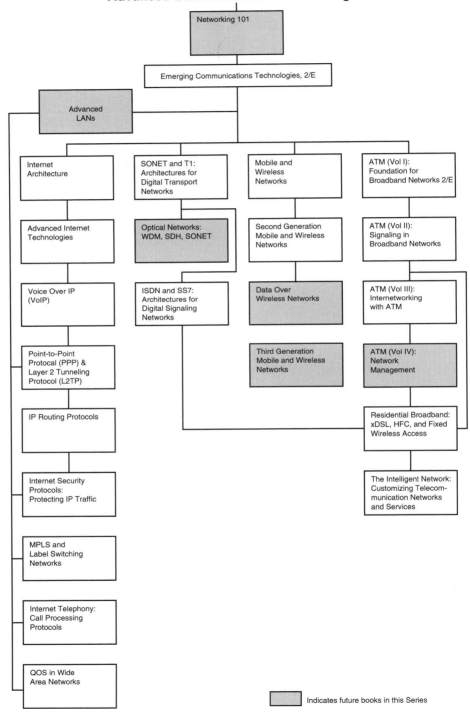

Networking 101

Emerging Communications Technologies, 2/E

Advanced LANs

Internet Architecture

SONET and T1: Architectures for Digital Transport Networks

Mobile and Wireless Networks

ATM (Vol I): Foundation for Broadband Networks 2/E

Advanced Internet Technologies

Optical Networks: WDM, SDH, SONET

Second Generation Mobile and Wireless Networks

ATM (Vol II): Signaling in Broadband Networks

Voice Over IP (VoIP)

ISDN and SS7: Architectures for Digital Signaling Networks

Data Over Wireless Networks

ATM (Vol III): Internetworking with ATM

Point-to-Point Protocol (PPP) & Layer 2 Tunneling Protocol (L2TP)

Third Generation Mobile and Wireless Networks

ATM (Vol IV): Network Management

IP Routing Protocols

Residential Broadband: xDSL, HFC, and Fixed Wireless Access

Internet Security Protocols: Protecting IP Traffic

The Intelligent Network: Customizing Telecommunication Networks and Services

MPLS and Label Switching Networks

Internet Telephony: Call Processing Protocols

QOS in Wide Area Networks

Indicates future books in this Series

MPLS and Label Switching Networks

UYLESS BLACK

Prentice Hall PTR
Upper Saddle River, New Jersey 07458
www.phptr.com

Library of Congress Cataloging-in-Publication Data

Black, Uyless D.
    MPLS and label switching networks / Uyless Black.
      p. cm.
    ISBN 0–13–015823–2
    1. Internet. 2. Computer networks—Management. 3.
    Telecommunication—Traffic—Management. 4. Packet switching (Date transmission) I.
    Title.

    TK5105.875.I57 .B55   2001
    004.6′6—dc21
                                     00–066564
                                        CIP

Acquisitions editor: *Mary Franz*
Editorial assistant: *Noreen Regina*
Cover designer: *Nina Scuderi*
Cover design director: *Jerry Votta*
Buyer: *Maura Zaldivar*
Marketing manager: *Dan DePasquale*
Project coordinator: *Anne Trowbridge*
Compositor/Production services: *Pine Tree Composition, Inc.*

© 2001 by Uyless Black
Published by Prentice Hall PTR
Prentice-Hall, Inc.
Upper Saddle River, New Jersey 07458

Prentice Hall books are widely used by corporations and government agencies for training, marketing, and resale.

The publisher offers discounts on this book when ordered in bulk quantities. For more information contact:

          Corporate Sales Department
          Phone: 800–382–3419
          Fax: 201–236–7141
          E-mail: corpsales@prenhall.com

          Or write:

          Prentice Hall PTR
          Corp. Sales Dept.
          One Lake Street
          Upper Saddle River, New Jersey 07458

Printed in the United States of America
10 9 8 7 6 5 4 3 2 1

ISBN: 0-13-015823-2

Prentice-Hall International (UK) Limited, *London*
Prentice-Hall of Australia Pty. Limited, *Sydney*
Prentice-Hall Canada Inc., *Toronto*
Prentice-Hall Hispanoamericana, S.A., *Mexico*
Prentice-Hall of India Private Limited, *New Delhi*
Prentice-Hall of Japan, Inc., *Tokyo*
Pearson Education Asia Pte. Ltd.
Editora Prentice-Hall do Brasil, Ltda., *Rio de Janeiro*

How can one make up an analogy of our everyday life, relating to the topic of label switching? Hardly anyone knows what label switching is, and yet if it did not exist, most of us would be very unhappy with our dealings with the Internet.

I asked some of my label switching impaired friends (everyone) about the term, and what thoughts came to their mind when they heard "label switching." Almost all of them told me their first thought was that of a person, lurking about in a store, switching labels on a product. I liked the idea, but it would not translate into an appropriate book cover, unless the subject was how to stop shoplifters.

So, I began to think about the basic premise of label switching in regard to writing a creature analogy.

The keystone of label switching is speed. It is designed to move traffic, say our email or voice conversations, rapidly from the sender to the receiver. It has other attractive attributes, explored later, but these attributes are not germane to this analogy.

After thinking about the idea of speed, the selection of the creature for this book cover was easy, the cheetah. It is the world's fastest land animal. Its speed is almost bewildering. It can accelerate from a dead-stop to 45 miles per hour in two seconds. It can run for about 300 yards at about 60 miles per hour. One recorded event clocked a cheetah at 71 miles per hour.

Label switching networks operate at considerably higher speeds. To use the cheetah analogy, they "run" on the order of thousands of miles per second.

But then, the label switching networks need not be concerned with things that attract the cheetah's attention when it is running, such as leg muscle movement, body movement, spine flexing to coordinate the legs and body, and a "few" other dynamics.

We could go on, but let's end the analogy with a salute to both: the remarkable speed of the cheetah, and the remarkable speed of label switching networks. The latter is the subject of this book.

Contents

CHAPTER 4   **MPLS Key Concepts**   **60**

CHAPTER 9   Constraint-Based Routing   174

CHAPTER 10   Other Key Concepts of MPLS   184

Preface

This book is one in a series of books called, "Advanced Communications Technologies." As the name of the book implies, the focus is on the switching of traffic though a network or networks. The term switching is also known in some parts of the industry as forwarding, relaying, and routing.

This book is an expansion of *Advanced Internet Technologies,* also part of this series.

I hope you find this book a valuable addition to your library.

ACKNOWLEDGMENTS

In many of my explanations of label switching operations, I have relied on the Internet Request for Comments (RFCs) and draft standards, published by the Internet Society, and I thank this organization for making the RFCs available to the public. The draft standards are "works in progress," and usually change as they wind their way to an RFC (if indeed they become an RFC). A work in progress cannot be considered final, but many vendors use them in creating products for the marketplace. Notwithstanding, they are subject to change.

For all the Internet standards and draft standards the following applies:

Copyright © The Internet Society (1998). All Rights Reserved.

1

Introduction

This chapter explains why label switching networks and Multiprotocol Label Switching (MPLS) have become key players in the emerging multiservice Internet. It explains the problems associated with conventional IP routing procedures and introduces the concepts of the alternative, label switching. The chapter also introduces the idea of quality of service (QOS) and explains its importance, as well as the importance of label switching to QOS. The chapter concludes with an example of a label switching and QOS network operation at a label switching router (LSR).

WHAT IS LABEL SWITCHING?

The basic concept of label switching is very simple. To show why, let's assume a user's traffic (say, an email message) is relayed from the user's computer to the recipient's computer. In traditional internets (those that do not use label switching), the method to relay this email is similar to postal mail: a destination address is examined by the relaying entity (for our work, a router; for the postal service, a mail person). This address determines how the router or mail person forwards the data packet or the mail envelope to the final recipient.

Label switching is different. Instead of using a destination address to make the routing decision, a number (a label) is associated with the packet. In the postal service analogy, a label value is placed on the envelope and is thereafter used in place of the postal address to route the mail to the recipient. In computer networks, a label is placed in a packet header and is used in place of an address (an IP address, usually), and the label is used to direct the traffic to its destination.

WHY USE LABEL SWITCHING?

Let's look at the reasons label switching is of such keen interest in the industry. We examine the topics of (a) speed and delay, (b) scalability, (c) simplicity, (d) resource consumption, and (e) route control.

Speed and Delay

Traditional software-based forwarding is too slow to handle the large traffic loads in the Internet or an internet, a topic explained in Appendix A. Even with enhanced techniques, such as a fast-table lookup for certain datagrams, the load on the router is often more than the router can handle. The result may be lost traffic, lost connections, and overall poor performance in an IP-based network.

Label switching, in contrast to IP forwarding, is proving to be an effective solution to the problem. The reason label switching is much faster is that the label value that is placed in an incoming packet header is used to access the forwarding table at the router; that is, the label is used to index the table. This lookup requires only one access to the table, in contrast to a traditional routing table access that might require several thousand lookups.

The result of this more efficient operation is that the user's traffic in the packet is sent though the network much more quickly than with the traditional IP forwarding operation, reducing the delay and response time to enact a transaction between users.

Jitter. For computer networks, speed and its nemesis, delay, has another component. It is the variability of the delay of the user traffic, due to the packet traversing several to many nodes in the network to reach its destination. It is also the accumulation of this variable delay as the packet makes its way from the sender to the receiver. At each node, the destination address in the packet must be examined and compared to a long list of potential destination addresses in the node's (usually a router) routing table.

As the packet traverses through these nodes, it encounters both delay and variable delay, depending on how long it takes for the table lookup and of course on the number of packets that must be processed in a given period. The end result, say at the receiving node, is jitter, an accumulation of the variable delays encountered at each node between the sender and the receiver.

This situation is onerous to speech packets because it often translates into uneven speech play-out to the person listening to the speech. It may even result in a person having to wait a few seconds to receive the final words of a sentence as the speech packets make their way through the network.

Once again, the more efficient label switching operation results in the user's traffic being sent through the network much more quickly and with less jitter than with the traditional IP routing operation.

Scalability

Certainly, speed is an important aspect of label switching, and processing the user traffic quickly in an internet is very important. But fast service is not all that label switching provides. It also can provide scalability. Scalability refers to the ability or inability of a system, in this case the Internet, to accommodate a large and growing number of Internet users. Thousands of new users (and supporting nodes, such as routers and servers) are signing on to the Internet each day. Imagine the task of a router if it has to keep track of all these users. Label switching offers solutions to this rapid growth and large networks by allowing a large number of IP addresses to be associated with one or a few labels. This approach reduces further the size of address (actually label) tables, and allows a router to support more users.

Simplicity

Another attractive aspect of label switching is that it is basically a forwarding protocol (or set of protocols, as we shall see). It is elegantly simple: forward a packet based on its label. How that label is ascertained is quite another matter; that is, how the control mechanisms are implemented to correlate the label to a specific user's traffic is irrelevant to the actual forwarding of the traffic. These control mechanisms are somewhat complex, but they do not affect the efficiency of the user traffic flow.

Why is this concept important? It means that a variety of methods may be employed to establish a label *binding* (an association) to the user's traffic. But after this binding has been accomplished, then label switching operations to forward the traffic are very simple. Label switching operations can be implemented in software, in ASIC, or in specialized processors.

Resource Consumption

The control mechanisms to set up the label must not be a burden to the network. They should not consume a lot of resources. If they do, then their benefits are largely negated. Fortunately, label switching networks do not need a lot of the network's resources to execute the control mechanisms to establish label switching paths for users' traffic (if they do consume a lot of resources, they are not designed well). We will spend quite a lot of time in this book describing the control mechanisms to support label switching.

Route Control (Control of the Forwarding Path)

With some exceptions, routing in internets is performed with the use of the IP destination address (or in a LAN, with the destination MAC address). Certainly, many products are available that use other information, such as the IP type of service (TOS) field and port numbers, as part of the forwarding decision. But destination-routing (the destination IP address) is the prevalent forwarding method.

Destination-routing is not always an efficient operation. To see why, consider Figure 1–1. Router 1 receives traffic from routers 2 and 3. If the IP destination address in the arriving IP datagram is for an address found at router 6, the routing table at router 1 directs the router to forward traffic to either router 4 or 5. With some exceptions, no other factor is involved.[1]

Label switching permits the routes through an internet to be subject to better control. For example, a labeled packet emanating from router 2 may be destined for an address at router 6; likewise, the same situation could hold for a labeled packet starting at router 3. However, the packets' different label values can instruct router 1 to send one labeled packet to router 4 and a packet with a different value to router 5.

This concept provides a tool to engineer the nodes and links to accommodate traffic more efficiently, as well as give certain classes of traffic

---

[1]Some vendors who manufacture routers, bridges, etc. have implemented their own proprietary alternatives to destination-based routing. Some products allow the network administrator to load-level traffic across more than one link; others use the TOS field, port numbers, and so on.

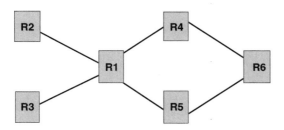

Figure 1–1   Destination-based routing.

(based on QOS needs) different levels of service. Perhaps the links between routers 1 and 4 and between 1 and 5 are DS3 and SONET respectively. This policy-based approach uses label switching to tailor the network to the needs of the traffic classes, a concept called *traffic engineering*.

Route Control Using IP

As noted, it is possible to use the TOS field and the precedence bits in this field to ameliorate some of the problems associated with destination-routing. However, the precedence bits are used in some networks and not used in others. While there are standards defining their use (the old RFC 791), a router may leave the bits untouched, or a router may alter them. A router may examine them, or a router may ignore them. Notwithstanding these comments, routers can be configured to use the precedence bits. Shortly, the use of these bits is described.

For this discussion, it is a good idea to reset these bits for all traffic entering your network from an unknown network. By resetting the precedence values, you guarantee that users who have set these bits to get special treatment (better service) do not receive this service at the expense of your internal network customers.

Policy-based Routing with IP.   Policy-based routing (PBR) is often associated with label switching protocols, such as Frame Relay, ATM, or MPLS. It can also be implemented with IP by using the TOS field as well as port numbers, the IP Protocol ID, or the size of the packets.

Using these fields allows the network provider to classify different types of traffic, preferably at the edge of the network; that is, the ingress to the network. Then the core routers can use the precedence bits to decide how to handle the incoming traffic. This "handling" can entail using different queues and different queuing methods.

IP policy-based routing also allows the network manager to execute a form of constraint-based routing, an operation explained in considerabel detail in this book. Based on the packet meeting or not meeting the criteria just discussed, policies can be executed that enable a router to:

- Set the precedence value in the IP header
- Set the next hop to route the packet (it need not be adjacent to the router)
- Set the output interface for the packet
- Set the next hop only if there is no route in the routing table

We should note that some of the literature in the industry states that IP, without label switching, is not capable of policy-based and constraint based routing. These claims are not accurate. The problem with the operations described in this section is not that they do not work; indeed they do. But the fact remains that the public Internet consists of many networks and many Internet Service Providers (ISPs), and there is no agreement among these parties on how to use the IP Precedence bits.

The same situation holds for label switching. Like IP precedence operations, label switching is only as effective as the agreements among network operators on how it is used.

THE ZIP CODE ANALOGY

To understand more about the basic ideas of label switching, let's return to the postal system example. As depicted in Figure 1–2(a), a piece of mail is being forwarded though the postal system from one party to another. Notice the actual address of the mail recipient is not used in the postal "network" to relay the envelope. Rather, the ZIP code 88888 is used as a label to identify where the mail is to go. After the envelope reaches its destination ZIP area (the end of the "postal path"), then the address (street number, etc.) is used to forward the mail to its intended reader.

This idea holds for label switching. In Figure 1–2(b), an IP datagram (packet) is sent to a label switching router for delivery to a destination IP address. The router appends a label to the packet (something like a ZIP code). Thereafter, the label, not the IP address, is used in the network to forward the traffic. Once the traffic has reached the end of the "label path," the IP address is used to make the final delivery to the end user.

Thus in both networks, the cumbersome addresses are not processed. This common sense approach saves a great deal of time and substantially

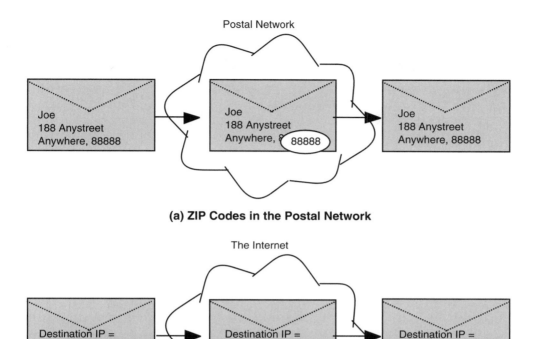

(a) ZIP Codes in the Postal Network

(b) Labels in the Internet

Figure 1–2   ZIP Codes and labels.

reduces the overhead of both the postal network and an internet. This reduction of time and overhead is the essence of label switching technology, an indispensable tool in today's internets. In later discussions, we will show more detailed examples of IP forwarding and label switching operations, and explain further why label switching is so effective.

A LABEL IS NOT AN ADDRESS

A label is not an address. It has no inherent topological significance. Moreover, until the label is correlated with an address, it has no routing significance. Therefore, a requirement still exists for conventional IP ad-

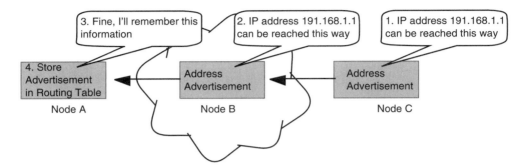

Figure 1–3   The address advertisement.

dress advertising, as shown in Figure 1–3. Part of the job of a label switching network is to correlate the addresses and routes with labels.

The routes are discovered by the IP routing protocols based on IP addresses. In this example, the label switching routers are advertising address 192.168.1.1. In most situations, an address prefix is advertised (a prefix is the network and subnetwork part of the 32-bit address), but that need not concern us for this general example.[2] This advertisement reaches the router on the left side of Figure 1–3. This router stores the routing information in its routing table. Thereafter, when the router receives a packet destined for address 191.168.1.1, it knows how to reach this address by consulting its routing table.

In a label switching network, an important job is to choose a label value to place onto the packet header for use in the network and to inform the other label switching routers about the association of the label value to the address. How this operation is accomplished is shown in a general way in Figure 1–4. Router A informs router B that address 191.168.1.1 is to be associated with label 88888. This association is called a *bind*.

When router B receives this label/address advertisement, it consults its routing table and looks up the next node that is to receive traffic destined for 191.168.1.1. As we learned in Figure 1–3, that next node is router C. Therefore, router B builds an entry in another table (called by

---

[2]The first part of this book uses complete 32-bit addresses. Later, examples of address prefixes are shown. Keep in mind that part of the value of the use of a label is to correlate one label value to multiple IP addresses. Thus, mapping labels to a prefix, and not an individual address, is the sensible way to use label switching. If you are not familiar with address prefixes, take a look at Appendix A.

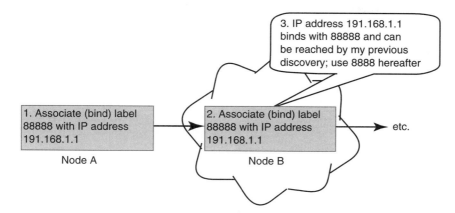

Figure 1–4   The label/address advertisement.

various names: label switching table, label mapping table, cross-connect table, as examples) that an incoming label from node A with a value of 88888 is to be routed onto the outgoing link to node C. This process continues until the packet reaches the final destination.

You may have noticed that I did not show the operations between router B and router C in Figure 1–3. The reason for this exclusion is that there are some additional operations between the LSRs B and C that are explained later.

The operation in Figure 1–4 has the label assigned by LSR A after it has discovered the path to the address. Another approach is for the binding to occur at the same time the address is advertised. Consequently, in Figure 1–5, the process of binding begins at node C. The label switching networks may support both approaches, and their pros and cons are explained in later chapters.

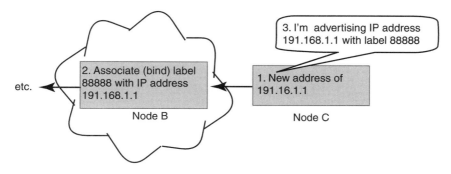

Figure 1–5   Advertising and binding at the same time.

HOW LABEL SWITCHING IS IMPLEMENTED
AND HOW IT CAME ABOUT

Several methods are employed to implement label switching. For this book, we examine those that are deployed and those under consideration, concentrating on the MPLS specifications. As we will see, many of them are similar. Chapter 3 provides a taxonomy of these methods.

The concept of label switching has been around for a number of years, and several firms developed proprietary label switching schemes for their products. These schemes are covered in a companion book to this series, *Advanced Internet Technologies,* and are explained in a general way in Chapter 3. For this book, the cogent aspect of this discussion is to emphasize that the implementation of these proprietary approaches provided a wealth of experience and information about label switching. But the proprietary schemes are not compatible. Therefore, the Internet Engineering Task Force (IETF) set up a working group to establish a standard for the label switching technology. This standard, not yet complete, is MPLS. We emphasize MPLS throughout this book with less emphasis on the proprietary label switching protocols, since the proprietary protocols will be replaced by MPLS.

CLARIFICATION OF TERMS

Later chapters explain the major responsibilities of internetworking units, such as label switching routers, but it is important to pause here and clarify some terms. Two protocols are employed by routers to successfully relay the user traffic to its receiver: (a) one protocol (say protocol 1) relays packets from a source user to a destination user, and (b) the other protocol (say protocol 2) finds a route for the packets to travel from the source to the destination.

Unfortunately, several terms are used to describe these two types of protocols, and the terms themselves are not models for clarity. Nonetheless, we must deal with them at the onset of our journey through label switching networks; otherwise, many parts of this book will be quite confusing. Figure 1–6 is used to explain these terms.

The older term to describe protocol 1 is *routing,* and the older terms to describe protocol 2 are *route advertising* or *route discovery.* These latter two terms are still used in the industry.

Today, as Figure 1–6 shows, the term *routing* is used to describe protocol 2, and the terms *forwarding* and *switching* are used to describe

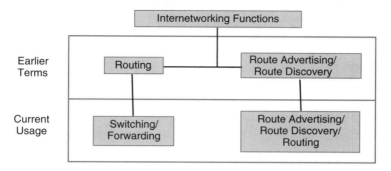

Figure 1–6   Terms and concepts.

protocol 1. In keeping with current industry practice, the new terms are used in this book. I will use route advertising, route discovery, and routing synonymously. However, I continue to use the term *routing table* or *label table* to describe the table of addresses or labels used to forward packets through the network.

To summarize, two protocols are involved in the internetworking process:

- Forwarding/Switching: Using a routing table or a label table to make a forwarding decision.
- Routing: Using route advertisements to acquire the knowledge to create the routing/label table that the forwarding protocol uses. For label switching networks, this advertising may entail the advertising of an address and its associated label.

THE NEED FOR A QOS-BASED INTERNET

The provisioning of adequate resources for an application (such as bandwidth for fast relay through the network) is not a simple process. Because of its complexity, internets in the past treated all applications' traffic alike and delivered the traffic on a best-effort basis, something like the postal service does for regular mail. That is, the traffic was delivered if the network had the resources to support the delivery. However, if the network became congested, the traffic was simply discarded. Some networks have attempted to establish some method of feedback (congestion control) to the user in order to request that the user reduce the infusion of traffic into the network. But as often as not, this technique is ineffective, because many traffic flows in data networks are very short, maybe just a few packets in a user-to-user session. So, by the time the user application receives the feedback, it is finished sending traffic. The feedback packets are worthless and have done nothing but create yet more traffic.

The best-effort concept means traffic is discarded randomly; no attempt is made to do any kind of intelligent traffic removal. This approach has the effect of discarding more packets from applications that have high bandwidth requirements and are placing more packets into the network than packets that have lesser requirements and are not sending as many packets into the network. So, the biggest "customers," those needing more bandwidth, are the very ones that are the most penalized! Assuming the customer who is supposedly given a bigger "pipe" to the network is paying more for that pipe, then it is reasonable to further assume that this customer should get a fair return on his or her investment.

It is charitable to say that the best-effort approach is not a very good model. What is needed is a way to manage the QOS based on the customer's requirements and investment.

Label Switching and QOS

In the past few years, it has become increasingly evident that internets need the ability to differentiate between types of traffic and to treat each type differently. We will have more to say shortly about this need, but for this discussion, we need first to define quality of service. The term was first used in the Open Systems Interconnection (OSI) reference model, and it refers to the ability of a service provider to support a user's application requirements with regard to bandwidth, latency (delay), jitter, and traffic loss. You may notice that these categories[3] are quite similar to the list of reasons for the use of label switching, discussed earlier.

The provision of bandwidth for an application means the network has sufficient capacity to support the application's throughput requirements, measured say, in packets per second.

The second service category is latency, which describes the time it takes to relay a packet from a sending node to a receiving node. Another term for latency is *round-trip time* (RTT), which is the time it takes to send a packet to a destination node and receive a reply from that node. RTT includes the transmission time in both directions and the processing time at the destination node. Applications, such as voice and video, have strict latency requirements. If the packet arrives too late, it is not useful

---

[3]Other QOS categories, such as security, pricing, and service agreements, are beyond the subject of this book.

and is ignored, resulting in wasted bandwidth and a reduction in the quality of the service to the application.

The third service category, jitter, is the variation of the delay between packets and usually occurs on an output link, where packets are competing for the router's outgoing links. Variable delay is onerous to speech. It complicates the receiver's job of playing out the speech image to the listener.

The last service category is packet loss. Packet loss is quite important in voice and video applications, since the loss may affect the outcome of the decoding process at the receiver and may also be detected by the end user's ears or eyes.

The Contribution of Label Switching

You might ask what label switching has to do with QOS. It does not have anything to do with certain aspects of the QOS categories, such as raw bandwidth. However, it was stated earlier that label switching can be a valuable tool to combat latency and jitter, two important quality of service operations for delay-sensitive traffic, such as video and voice. Since label switching is designed to speed up the relaying of traffic in an internet, it follows that the technology will reduce latency and improve jitter. Indeed, an internet that does not use label switching runs the risk of experiencing unacceptable QOS performance for delay-sensitive traffic.

Of course, label switching unto itself will not solve the delay and variable delay problems that are systemic to data networks. If we are connected to a low-bandwidth network, label switching is not going to give us more bandwidth, but I am stating label switching will ameliorate delay and jitter problems significantly.

LABEL SWITCHING'S LEGACY: X.25 AND VIRTUAL CIRCUITS

We take a change of pace here and look at a bit of history. The label switching concept began with X.25. In the late 1960s and early 1970s, many data communications networks were created by companies, government agencies, and other organizations. The design and programming of these networks were performed by each organization to fulfill specific business needs. During this time, an organization had no reason to adhere to any common convention for its data communications protocols since the organization's private network provided services only to itself. Consequently, these networks used specialized protocols that were tailored to satisfy the organization's requirements.

During this period, several companies and telephone administrations in the U.S., Canada, and Europe implemented a number of *public data networks* based on packet switching concepts. These systems were conceived to provide a service for data traffic that paralleled the telephone system's service for voice traffic.

But they did not nail up bandwidth like the telephone system. Indeed, X.25 represented a major change in viewing service to a user: use a best-effort approach but allow the user to request certain levels of service.

The public network vendors were faced with answering a major question: How can the network best provide the interface for a user's terminal or computer to the network? The potential magnitude of the problem was formidable because each terminal or computer vendor had developed its own set of data communications protocols. Indeed, some companies, such as IBM, had developed scores of different protocols within their own product lines.

X.25 came about largely because these nascent networks recognized that a common network interface protocol was needed, especially from the perspective of the network service providers.

In 1974, the (former) CCITT issued the first draft of X.25 (the "Gray Book"). It was revised in 1976, 1978, 1980, and again in 1984 with the publication of the "Red Book" recommendation. Until 1988, X.25 was revised and republished every four years. In 1988, the ITU-T announced its intention to publish changes to its recommendations (including X.25) as they were warranted, rather than in the four-year cycle previously utilized.

The Logical Channel Number: Precursor to the Label

X.25 identifies each packet in the network with a logical channel number (LCN). The LCN is used to distinguish the different users' traffic that are operating on the same physical link. This idea is to mask from the user the fact that the link is being shared by other users, thus the term *virtual circuit* (you think you have the full bandwidth of the link, but you don't). A virtual circuit and its *label,* the logical channel number, is quite similar to the modern label switching network. But there are differences that will be pointed out as we move into the details of label switching networks.

Frame Relay and ATM: A Rose by any Other Name is Still a Rose

The successors to X.25, Frame Relay and ATM, also use the virtual circuit concept. For Frame Relay, the virtual circuit IDs are called data link connection IDs (DLCIs); for ATM they are called virtual path IDs/virtual channel IDs (VPIs/VCIs). Regardless of their names, they are (a) virtual circuit IDs, and (b) label values.

MPLS networks must interwork with these networks, since they are quite prevalent as the principal bearer of services for wide area internets. Fortunately, the MPLS labels correlate rather easily with the ATM and Frame Relay labels, and later chapters explore this subject in considerable detail.

MPLS: STATUS AND CONCEPTS

Work is underway to develop the Multiprotocol Label Switching technology. As of this writing, it is not yet finished, and you may wish to obtain the Internet Draft document http://www.ietf.org for more details. The following discussion reflects the latest status of MPLS, but the final specification will reflect changes, although they will probably be minor.

MPLS is a label swapping (mapping) and forwarding technology, but it integrates label swapping with network layer routing. Label swapping, or mapping, means the changing of the label value in the packet header as the packet moves from one node to another, and the rationale for this operation is explained in chapters 2 and 3.

The idea of MPLS is to improve the performance of network layer routing, and the scalability of the network layer. An additional goal is to provide greater flexibility in the delivery of routing services (by allowing new routing services to be added without a change to the forwarding paradigm). MPLS does not make a forwarding decision with each L_3 datagram, but uses a concept called the functional equivalence class (FEC). An FEC is associated with a class of datagrams; the class depends on a number of factors, such as the destination address and the type of traffic in the datagram (voice, data, fax, etc.). Based on the FEC, a label is then negotiated between neighbor LSRs from the ingress to the egress of a routing domain. As we showed earlier, the label is then used to relay the traffic through the network.

The initial MPLS efforts of the Working Group focus on IPv4 and IPv6. The core technology can be extendible to multiple network layer protocols, such as IPX, and SNA. However, there is little interest in expanding MPLS to other network layer protocols, since IP is by far the most pervasive.

The basic idea is not to restrict MPLS to any specific link layer technology, such as ATM or Frame Relay. Most of the efforts so far are directed to the interworking of MPLS and ATM, but in the future, it is quite conceivable that MPLS could operate directly with IP over the physical layer, and not use ATM at all.

In addition, MPLS does not require one specific label distribution protocol (agreeing on the use of label values between neighbor LSRs). It assumes there may be more than one, such as RSVP, BGP, or the Label Distribution Protocol (LDP). Considerable attention is on LDP, since is it being designed from scratch for MPLS networks. Other protocols, such as BGP and RSVP, are also very good methods for label distribution.

EXAMPLES OF LABEL AND QOS RELATIONSHIPS

We have learned that the label is used for forwarding operations—to determine how to relay the packet to a next node. We also learned that it can be used to determine the services that will be provided to the packet during its journey through the network. Thus, the label may be associated with the packet's QOS support. The words "may be" must be emphasized because some MPLS implementations use the label to make forwarding decisions and use another field in the packet to determine how the packet is treated; that is, what kind of QOS it receives.

Figure 1–7 shows how two packets are processed at an LSR, and the relationships of QOS and label operations. The packets, identified with labels 30 and 70, are sent to the switch's interface from an upstream node (say, another router, not shown in this figure). The labels are then used to access a label switching table. The two table entries for labels 30 and 70 are shown at the bottom of the figure.

Each table entry contains the label number and the associated ingress interface number: 30.a and 70.a for these two packets. The ingress interface is the communications link interface into the router. The table information is associated with the profile conformance entries and is used to monitor the flow associated with each of these packets. These profile examples are usually relevant to the first switch in the QOS domain; that is, at the user-to-network interface (UNI). They determine if the packet flow is conforming or nonconforming to the service level agreement (SLA).[4] The profile for flow 30 is a burst tolerance (BT)

---

[4]The SLA is a contract between the network provider and the customer. It stipulates the QOS that the provider is supposed to provide, including services not described in this book, such as security, management reports, and penalties for nonconformance to the SLA contract.

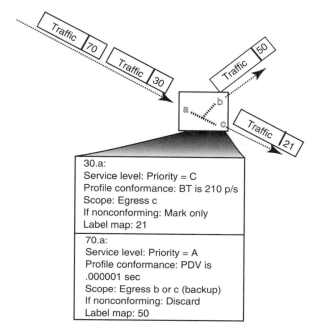

Figure 1–7   Labels and associated QOS operations.

of 210 packets per second (210 p/s); the profile for flow 70 is a packet delay variation (PDV) of no greater than 1 microsecond.

The service level entries in the tables also reveal how the packet is to be treated if the traffic for each flow adheres to its SLA. This example uses priorities to differentiate the treatments. Priority = C is for asynchronous traffic, and priority = A identifies synchronous, real-time traffic. The priorities in the example are relative; priority C is not as high as A.

Another entry in the table is the scope of service, shown as "Scope" in the figure. The service for these two packets is scoped to the switch's egress interfaces, the router's output link interfaces. If the services for these packets are end-to-end, perhaps through multiple QOS domains, the ingress and egress must be provisioned at each node that resides in the QOS region. Therefore, we can assume in this example that these egress ports are provisioned with an end-to-end path in mind. Notice that packet 70 is scoped to two egress interfaces, b and c. This approach enables the packet to be routed to the link that is experiencing better performance, or routed around network failures.

Another entry in the table reflects the operations that are to be performed on the packet if its flow is nonconforming to the SLA conformance profile. Packet 30 will be marked (tagged) if it is nonconforming. "Mark only" means the packet is not to be discarded (unless the switch is in a precipitous situation). The tag will relegate the service on the packet flow to a lesser quality of service. Packet 70 belongs to a synchronous real-time flow, so if it is nonconforming, it is discarded.

The last entry in the tables is the label that is placed in the packet header for transmittal out of the egress interface to the next node. Label 30 is mapped to label 21, and label 70 is mapped to label 50. The term *map* is also called a *swap*. So, label swapping is the changing of the label value at the LSR. Label swapping is quite important in label switching networks and is explained in chapters 2 and 3.

DETERMINATION OF THE PHYSICAL PATH THROUGH THE NETWORK: THE LABEL SWITCHED PATH

The path through a label switched network is determined in one of two ways. With the first, traditional routing protocols (such as OSPF or BGP) are used to discover IP addresses (also called prefixes in this book). This information, the next node to an address, is correlated to a label, yielding a label switched path (LSP). Second, the LSP can be set up (configured manually) based on the idea of constraint-based routing (CR). This approach may use a routing protocol to assist in setting up the LSP, but the LSP is "constrained" by other factors, such as the need to provide a certain QOS level. Indeed, delay-sensitive traffic is the prime candidate for constraint-based routing. Chapters 7 and 8 are devoted to this subject.

SUMMARY

Traditional IP forwarding is too slow to handle the large traffic loads in the Internet or an internet. Even with enhanced techniques, such as a fast-table lookup for certain datagrams, the load on the router is often more than the router can handle. The result may be lost traffic, lost connections, and overall poor performance in the IP-based network. Label switching, in contrast to IP forwarding, is proving to be an effective solution to the problem. The main attributes of label switching are fast relay of the traffic, scalability, simplicity, and route control.

MPLS represents a vendor-independent specification for label switching. It is designed to improve the performance of network layer routing and the scalability of the network layer. An additional goal is to provide greater flexibility in the delivery of routing services.

2

Label Switching Basics

This chapter introduces the basic concepts of label switching. The functional equivalence class (FEC), introduced in Chapter 1, is explained in more detail. The information that makes up an FEC, as well as how an edge router associates the FEC with a label and a class of service, is described.

Label allocation methods are examined, with examples of local and remote binding, upstream and downstream binding, and control and data binding operations. The concept of a label space is introduced, and examples of how labels are set up between neighbor routers are provided.

THE FUNCTIONAL EQUIVALENCE CLASS

The term FEC is applied to label switching operations. FEC is used to describe an association of discrete packets with a destination address, usually the final recipient of the traffic, such as a host machine. FEC implementations may also associate an FEC value with a destination address and a class of traffic. The class of traffic is typically associated with a destination port number.

Why is FEC used? First, it allows the grouping of packets into classes. From this grouping, the FEC value in a packet can be used to set priorities for the handling of the packets, giving higher priority to certain FECs over others. FECs can be used to support efficient QOS operations. For example, FECs can be associated with high-priority, real-time voice traffic, low-priority newsgroup traffic, and so on.

The matching of the FEC with a packet is achieved by using a label to identify a specific FEC. For different classes of service, different FECs and their associated labels are used. For Internet traffic, the following identifiers are candidate parameters for establishing an FEC. In some systems, only the destination IP address is used.

- Source and/or destination IP addresses
- Source and/or destination port numbers
- IP Protocol ID (PID)
- IPv4 Differentiated Services (DS) Codepoint
- IPV6 flow label

Scalability and Granularity

The network administrator has control over how big the forwarding tables become by implementing FEC course granularity. If only the destination address is used for the FEC (and of course address prefixes are used; see Appendix A), the tables can be kept to a manageable size. Yet this course granularity does not provide a way to support classes of traffic and QOS operations. On the other hand, a network supporting fine granularity by using port numbers and PIDs will have more traffic classifications, more FECs, more labels, and a larger forwarding table. This network will likely not scale to a large user base.

Fortunately, label switching networks need not be one or the other. A combination of course and fine granularity FECs is permissible.

Information Used in the Forwarding Decision

Keep in mind that whatever the terms used, the focus of label switching is the *forwarding of a packet to its final destination*. And as we learned, the operations may base their forwarding decisions on one or more fields in the incoming packet. These fields are listed here (in more detail than in the list above) and depicted in Figure 2–1. You will note that some of the information explained in this section was not listed above. The reason is that some of these values are used by a router, a switch, or a bridge to make forwarding decisions, but they are usually not used for the FEC.

- Layer 2
  (a) A LAN address (the IEEE MAC address)
  (b) An ATM or Frame Relay virtual circuit ID (VCID)
- Layer 3
  (a) Destination and source IP addresses (or some other layer 3 address, such as IPX, Appletalk, etc.)
- Layer 4
  (a) Destination and source port numbers
- IP Protocol ID

The reason that port numbers and the IP Protocol may be used in the FEC and the forwarding decision process is that these fields (the destination port number and the PID) identify the type of traffic residing in the IP datagram payload. For example, the PID may be coded by the transmitter of the original datagram to indicate that the payload is OSPF traffic. A router can be programmed to treat this traffic differently than if the PID indicated the payload was, say, TCP or UDP traffic. If indeed the payload contains TCP or UDP traffic, the port numbers in the TCP or UDP header then indicate what type of TCP or UDP payload resides in the remainder of the packet. For example, the destination port number might be coded to indicate the traffic is voice, email, file transfer, and so on. Thus, these fields become quite important for networks that

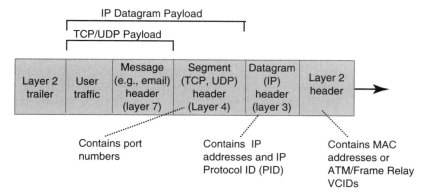

Figure 2-1　The information used in forwarding decisions.

need to support different QOS services for different kinds of traffic; that is, fine granularity.

The MPLS label is not shown in Figure 2–1, unless it is the ATM or Frame Relay VCID. Another header, called a *shim header,* may exist in the packet and is explained shortly.

LABEL ALLOCATION METHODS

The assignment of the value to a packet varies, depending on the vendor's approach and/or the standard employed (an Internet RFC, or Working Draft). This part of the chapter introduces the concepts of label allocation (binding), and in later discussions, we focus on a more detailed examination.

Local and Remote Binding

The term binding refers to an operation at a label switching router (LSR) in which a label is associated with an FEC. As shown in Figure 2–2, local label allocation (local binding) refers to the operation in which the local router sets up a label relationship with an FEC. The router can set this relationship up as it receives traffic, or it can set it up as it receives control information from an upstream or downstream neighbor. Remote binding is an operation in which a neighbor node assigns a binding to the local node. Typically, this is performed with control messages, such as a label distribution message.

Downstream and Upstream Binding

As depicted in Figure 2–3, downstream label allocation refers to a method where the label allocation is done by the downstream LSR. The term *downstream* refers to the direction in which a user packet is sent. When the upstream router (Ru) sends a packet to the downstream router (Rd), the packet has been identified previously as a member of an FEC and the label (say, label L) is associated with the FEC. Thus, L is Ru's outgoing label, and L is Rd's incoming label.

Figure 2–2   Local and remote bindings.

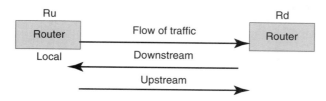

Figure 2–3   Upstream and downstream binding.

Control Binding versus Data-Driven Binding

The broad category of control versus data-driven, or flow-driven, binding is distinguished as follows. Control binding is set up in advance with control messages (a label distribution protocol) or using craft commands (provisioning) at the node. Data (or flow control) binding occurs dynamically, based on an analysis of the streaming packets. These ideas are illustrated in Figure 2–4.

In most systems, both concepts are used together. First, a binding is established between two nodes through the use of a label distribution protocol to associate an FEC with a label. Then, as the packets arrive at an LSR node (usually the ingress node to the label switching network), the contents of the packet that are germane to the FEC are examined. The relevant label value is then fetched from a table and placed in the label header of the packet.

LABEL SPACE AND LABEL ASSIGNMENTS

Labels can be assigned between LSRs by one of two methods. In explaining this idea, the term *label space* refers to the way in which the label is associated with an LSR. Figure 2–5 illustrates these ideas.

The first method is a *per interface label space*. Labels are associated with a specific interface on an LSR, such as a DS3 or SONET interface.

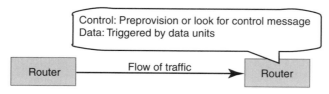

Figure 2–4   Control vs. data/flow driven binding.

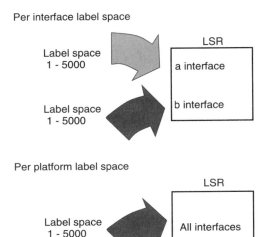

Figure 2–5   Label space and label assignments.

Common implementations of this method are ATM and Frame Relay networks, where virtual circuit ID labels are associated with an interface. This approach is used only when two peers are directly connected over an interface, and the label is only used to identify traffic sent on one interface. If the LSR uses an interface value to keep track of the labels on each interface, a label value can be reused at each interface. In a sense, this interface identifier becomes an *internal* label in the LSR for the *external* label sent between the LSRs.

The second method is a *per platform label space*. Here, incoming labels are shared across all interfaces attached to the node. This means the node (such as a host or an LSR) must allocate the label space across all interfaces. The choice for these methods is implementation-specific, although the per interface label space allocation method is more common as of this writing.

THE EDGE ROUTER AND THE LABEL SWITCHING DOMAIN

Figure 2–6 shows three LSRs (switches A, B, and C) and two host machines, with addresses 191.168.1.2 and 191.168.1.1. LSRs A and B are called edge routers (or edge LSRs) because they sit at the edge of the label switching internet, shown in the figure as the label switching domain.

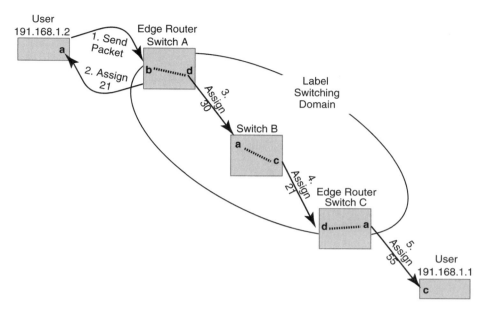

Figure 2–6   Label assignments.

This domain may consist of one or more physical networks. The domain's boundaries are set up by network administrators. For this example, the two host machines are not part of the label switching domain. This means the hosts do not execute any label switching operations unless they are initiated by the edge LSRs. They communicate with conventional IP addresses (shown as 191.168.1.1 and 191.168.1.2), but in this example their traffic flows are indeed assigned labels by the edge LSRs. These hosts may reside on a local area network at a business site, or they be connected to the routers through conventional dial-up links.

The user node at the top part of the figure sends a packet to LSR A in event 1. This packet is examined for the relevant fields that make up the FEC. Based on this examination, LSR A makes decisions about how to treat this packet. If it is to be subject to label operations, the LSR notifies host 191.168.1.2 in event 2 by assigning a label (number 21) to the FEC flow, an example of a downstream binding operation in that the downstream node is assigning the label to the flow. Events 3, 4, and 5 show upstream bindings. These bindings take place through label distribution protocols, a topic discussed in chapters 5, 6, and 10.

The notations in Figure 2–5 of a, b, c, and d represent the ingress and egress interfaces on the machines, such as a SONET or DS1 link. In this example, labels are associated with a specific interface on each node.

Roles of Hosts and LSRs

The host machines in this example are likely not end user machines, such as PCs or work stations. Most likely, they are local routers or servers that sit between a company's network and the edge LSRs. In this regard, they are somewhat passive in the label switching operations, although the label switching software must be present in these machines. This practice emanates from ATM and Frame Relay networks, in which the labels are assigned by the network provider's switches, and sent to the customer's local routers or switches.

EXAMPLES OF FEC AND LABEL CORRELATIONS: THE LABEL SWITCHING TUNNEL

This example is extended by referring back to the example in Chapter 1 (Figure 1–2). In Figure 2–7, the packet is sent to the edge router; this router examines the FEC-related fields in the headers. It decides to assign a label to this packet as well as treat the packet in a certain way, such as forwarding the packet to an output queue. The packet is encapsulated into an outer packet, and the header of the outer packet has label number 88888 placed in it.

This idea is called a *label switching tunnel*, which means the inner packet is not examined by the internal LSRs within the network. Their only concern is the processing of the outer packet header's label and han-

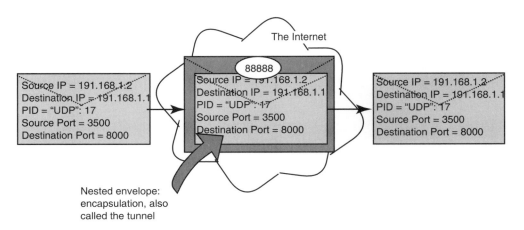

Figure 2–7 The label switching tunnel.

dling the packet accordingly. At the egress node, the packet is decapsulated (detunnelled), and the destination IP address, along with the other identifiers, is used to determine how the packet is treated at the receiving node.

ALTERNATIVES FOR CARRYING THE LABEL

In order to explain basic label switching concepts, the previous explanations have been somewhat generic in depicting the tunnel and the contents of the tunneled packet. Figure 2–8 shows a more specific example of a packet that contains a label. The label can reside in one or two headers in the packet. It may reside in the header of the layer 2 bearer services protocol, such as ATM or Frame Relay, or it may reside in a special shim header that follows the layer 2 header and precedes the layer 3 (IP) header, or it may reside in both headers, a topic discussed in later chapters.

The choice of how the label is represented in the packet depends on several factors. The principal factor is whether the packet is transported through ATM or Frame Relay. If this transport occurs, the label can reside in the virtual circuit fields in the ATM or Frame Relay headers. If the packet is not transported through these networks, a separate header is used to contain the label.

LABEL SWAPPING

The label (with rare exceptions) does not remain the same value as the packet is transported through the label switching domain. Typically, each LSR accepts the incoming packet and changes the value of the label before it sends the packet to the next node in the routing path. The operation is called label swapping (sometimes label mapping).

Figure 2–9 shows the entries in the LS tables for one label switching path (LSP) between users 191.168.1.2 and 191.168.1.1. For this discussion, the path is identified with:

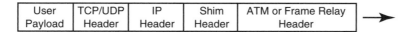

Figure 2–8   Alternatives for carrying the label.

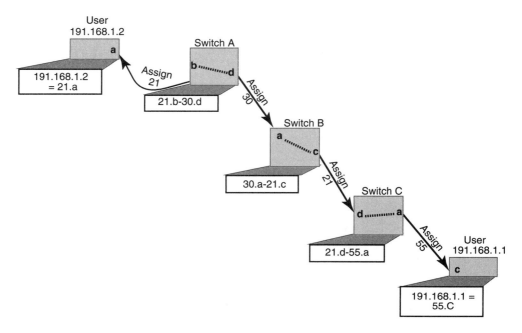

Figure 2–9   Label swapping.

- Label 21: Identifies the LSP between user 191.168.1.2 and switch A
  21.a: is the output interface at 191.168.1.2
  21.b: is the input interface at switch A
- Label 30: Identifies the LSP between switch A and switch B
  30.d: is the output interface at switch A
  30.a: is the input interface at switch B
- Label 21: Identifies the LSP between switch B and switch C
  21.c: is the output interface at switch B
  21.d: is the input interface at switch C
- Label 55: Identifies the LSP between switch C and user 191.168.1.1
  55.a :   is the output interface at switch C
  55.c: is the input interface at 191.168.1.1

Several observations are noteworthy about this figure. First, there must be some means to associate the labels with the FEC, and the association must be made at each machine that participates in the end-to-end LSP.

Second, in this example, the label is correlated with the sender's outgoing interface and the receiver's incoming interface, a point made earlier. Since the labels are so associated, they can be reused at each interface on the switches or user machines. In a sense, the interface numbers in the switch act as *internal* labels for the connection.

Third, the selection of the labels is a matter between the user and its adjacent switch, or between adjacent switches. Consequently, there is no requirement to keep the labels unambiguous across interfaces and through the network. For example, label 21 is used twice, between 191.168.1.2 and switch A, and then between switches B and C. Trying to manage universal label values across multiple nodes and different networks would not be a very pleasant task.

Fourth, the example shows the label bindings (the association of the labels between nodes) in one direction only. It is a straightforward task to use the LS table in a bidirectional manner. For example, if the traffic were flowing from switch C to switch B, the LS table would appear as

- Label 21: Identifies the path between switch C and switch B
    - d: is the output interface at switch C
    - c: is the input interface at switch B

However, some label switching implementations do not allow a label operation to be bidirectional. This means a two-way connection must have a set of bindings for each direction of the connection.

SUMMARY

This chapter introduced the basic concepts of label switching. The functional equivalence class (FEC), introduced in Chapter 1, was explained in more detail. The information that makes up an FEC, and defines how an edge router associates the FEC with a label and a class of service, was described.

Label allocation methods were examined, with examples of local and remote binding, upstream and downstream binding, and control and data binding operations. The concept of a label space was introduced, and examples were provided of how the labels are set up between neighbor routers.

3

Switching and Forwarding Operations

One of the most confusing aspects of switching, routing, and forwarding technologies is discerning exactly what these terms mean. Vendors, standards groups, and service providers often attach different meanings to these terms. We have already dealt with the differences between routing and forwarding (Chapter 1, see Figure 1–6). In this chapter, we clarify the concepts of switching and forwarding by providing a taxonomy of the subject.

Some of the examples in this chapter are proprietary, and some will fade away as MPLS becomes more prevalent. Also, I include quite a lot of material on Cisco's tag switching protocol for two reasons. First, it provides a good example of an actual label switching implementation, and second, it forms the basis for many of the MPLS operations.

A TAXONOMY OF SWITCHING AND FORWARDING NETWORKS

Initially, the term *routing* referred to making relaying decisions that were performed in a machine typically based with software programs and routing tables stored in conventional RAM. In contrast, *switching* referred to relaying decisions with the support functions consisting principally in hardware with specialized processors.

Furthermore, routing traditionally referred to using a destination layer 3 address (for example, an IP address) to make the relaying decisions, whereas switching traditionally referred to using a layer 2 address to perform the relaying operations. In many instances, the layer 2 address was (and still is) a 48-bit IEEE Media Access Control (MAC) address used in local area networks. For layer 3 operations, the address traditionally has been the IP address.

However, in the past few years a number of technologies have emerged that use these techniques or combinations of these techniques and append different names to them. The most common names currently in the industry are described in this chapter. Be aware that many of these techniques are quite similar to each other, and some of them have overlapping functions. As stated, these overlaps make for a confusing mix of techniques.

Figure 3–1 should help you during this discussion. We will examine each of the entries in Figure 3–1, starting at the top left part of the taxonomy, and work our way across and down.

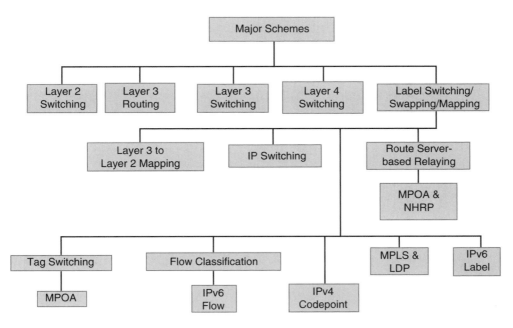

Figure 3–1   A taxonomy for switching and forwarding protocols.

Information Used in the Forwarding Decision

Keep in mind that whatever the terms used, the focus of the taxonomy is the *sending of a packet to its final destination*. In addition, the operations described in this chapter base their forwarding decisions on one or more fields in the incoming packet. These fields are described in Chapter 2; see Figures 2–1 and 2–8.

LAYER 2 SWITCHING

Figure 3–2 should be studied during the discussions on layer 2 switching and layer 3 routing (forwarding), the subjects of the next two sections in this chapter.

A LAN *bridge* operates at layer 2, the data link layer (always at the MAC sublayer and sometimes at the LLC sublayer). Typically, it uses 48-bit MAC addresses to perform its relaying functions. The term *layer 2 switching* is often used to describe a LAN bridge.

However, this term is also used to describe an ATM or Frame Relay switch. Since ATM and Frame Relay operate at layer 2, they fit into the category of L_2 switching protocols. Strictly speaking, ATM and Frame Relay should be considered as a combination of L_3 and L_2 switching technologies because both were derived from X.25, which uses a layer 3 header for its principal operations. But most people in the industry use the term L_2 switching for ATM and Frame Relay, so I will defer to this practice.

If ATM or Frame Relay is employed, their virtual circuit IDs (VCIDs) are used to make the forwarding decision. The VCIDs are really labels, although they are managed differently than MPLS labels, a subject discussed later in this book.

LAYER 3 ROUTING (ACTUALLY FORWARDING)

This operation uses a conventional router and forwards the traffic based on a 32-bit IP destination address that resides in the IP header. IP is classified as a layer 3 protocol, thus the term layer 3 routing.

However, it is important that the term routing be clarified once again. In Chapter 1 (see Figure 1–6), we emphasized that routing is now associated with route advertisements and route discovery. Consequently, if you read a recent RFC that explains a routing protocol, the reference is to protocols such as OSPF and BGP, and not to IP.

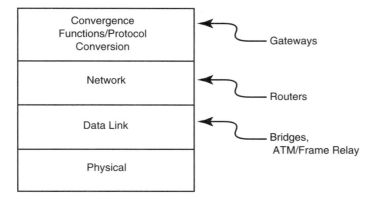

(a) Protocol Layer Placement:

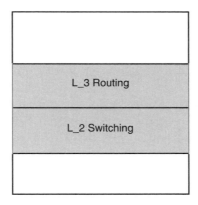

(b) Traditional Routing/Switching:

Figure 3–2   Bridges, routers, gateways, and others.

Problem with IP Forwarding Operations

Traditional IP forwarding operations are fraught with overhead. When the destination address in the IP datagram header is examined by a router, it must match this address against a routing table to determine the next hop to the destination. This operation may require the search of a very large routing table; at major peering points in the Internet, the table is about 50,000 entries. Each incoming packet must be processed against this table. In addition, the use of subnet masks require the destination IP address in the incoming packet to be matched against the mask (prefix) in the routing table. The longest match rule requires that the route chosen is based on a mask that yields the most matching bits, a topic beyond this book, but explained in a companion book to this series, *IP Routing Protocols*. The result is that conventional IP forwarding simply does not work in large internets. It takes too long to process a packet.

LAYER 3 SWITCHING

This technology is a newer method of packet forwarding. The distinguishing attribute of layer 3 switching is that the relay functions are performed in hardware through the use of applications-specific integrated circuits (ASIC), or specially designed hardware. They differ from some of the other implementations just discussed in that they do not perform any label mapping nor do they necessarily rely on ATM/Frame Relay-based switching fabrics. The IP address is used without regard to any tag or label.

Cache Assisting Switching

Some layer 3 switching systems use cache assisted switching. A cache is built for datagrams containing addresses for specific networks that receive a lot of traffic. With this approach, each datagram is not subject to the conventional reliance on a central table for the route lookup. The most frequently accessed routes are stored in the high-speed cache.

Distributed Switching

With distributed switching, a separate processor is placed on each interface module. The routing table is calculated by a central processor, but the processor does not become involved with the forwarding decisions for each datagram. Instead, the forwarding tables are downline-loaded to the interface processors. In turn, these processors make the forwarding decisions.

Example of Layer 3 Switching

An example of a layer 3 switch is a multigigabit router (MGR) built by BBN technologies (see "A 50-Gb/s Router," by Craig Partridge et al., *IEEE ACM Transactions on Networking,* Vol. 6, No. 3, June 1998).

Figure 3–3 shows the overall architecture for the MGR. We will assume the packets enter the router from the left and exit to the right. The router contains multiple line cards, which support one or more interfaces, and forwarding engine cards, all connected to a switch. The arriving packet has its header removed and passed through the switch to the forwarding engine card, while the other part of the packet is stored on the incoming line card. The forwarding engine examines the header, determines the routing for the packet, updates the header, and forwards it back to the incoming line card, with associated forwarding information. Then, this line card appends the revised header to the other part of the packet and sends the reconstituted packet to the appropriate outgoing line card. The MGR has a total capacity of 50 Gb/s. Its packets per second rate (PPS) is cited at 32 million PPS.

The MGR uses several approaches that are quite different from conventional routers. First, the router uses distributed routing tables, introduced earlier. Each forwarding engine has a complete set of tables instead of a limited subset of addresses, as found in some routers. This approach avoids the time delay and possible contention in using one central table. Moreover, these tables do not contain all the entries found in conventional tables; they contain only next-hop information.

Second, the switch is not a shared bus, but rather a point-to-point switch containing 15 ports. The switch is an input-queued fabric. Each input maintains a FIFO, and uses a protocol to bid for the output. This approach avoids the head-of-line blocking, and the designers state that they have achieved 100 percent throughput.

Third, the forwarding engines are on separate line cards. This approach gives more "real estate" for both functions and allows the design-

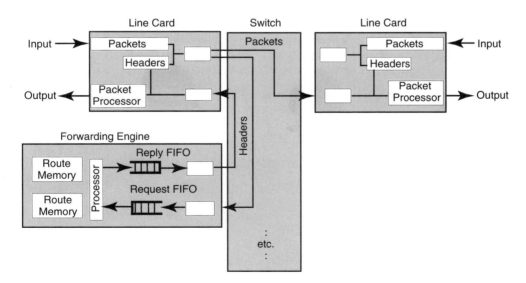

Figure 3–3   A layer 3 switch.

ers more flexibility in allocating how many interfaces will share a forwarding engine. Also, it is possible to dedicate a single forwarding engine to a single virtual network, which can simplify configuration and maintenance operations.

Fourth, the line cards are able to accept different L_2 protocol data units, but they must be able to translate them into a common internal L_2 format for processing inside the MGR.

Fifth, the router supports QOS operations. The approach is for the forwarding engine to classify the packet and assign the packet to a flow. This information is passed to the output line card, which schedules the packet transmission with a special QOS processor.

LAYER 4 SWITCHING

Layer 4 switching is a relatively new term. It refers to an operation that examines the Internet port numbers as part of a forwarding decision. The destination port number is certainly used; the source port number may be used. The port numbers are used in conjunction with the source (maybe) and destination (most likely) IP address to make a forwarding decision. In addition, the Protocol ID (PID) field in the IP header may also be used. Therefore, layer 4 switching is really not just layer 4 switching. The forwarding operation uses other information as well, an idea explained in Chapter 2 (see Figure 2–1).

LABEL SWITCHING/SWAPPING/MAPPING

The remainder of the taxonomy consists of various renditions of label switching. I title this part of the taxonomy "Label Switching/Swapping/Mapping" to cover the terms used for the operation. Let's take a look at each of these procedures. As you proceed through this book, you will see that MPLS includes many of these "individual" procedures, but not all of them.

LAYER 3 TO LAYER 2 MAPPING

This approach is similar to flow classification and IP switching, with the layer 3 address being mapped to a label or virtual circuit ID. While this example (see Figure 3–4) shows only the mapping of the layer 3 ad-

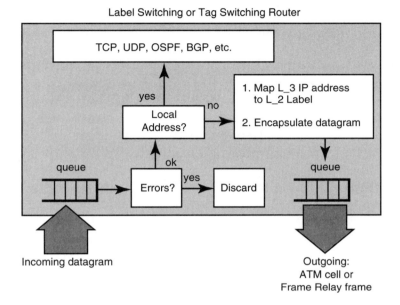

Label Switching or Tag Switching Router

Figure 3–4   Layer 3 to layer 2 mapping at the ingress LSR.

dress, the operation can also use Internet port numbers and the PID to derive an FEC for the mapping procedure.

The address (or FEC) mapping can be to the ATM virtual circuit ID (a virtual path/virtual channel ID (VPI/VCI) or a Frame Relay virtual circuit ID (a data link connection ID (DLCI), or for that matter, an MPLS label or a Cisco tag. The mapping typically occurs by a router or switch that sits at the edge of the network. Implementations for this method are fairly widespread, including Cisco's tag switching, IBM's ARIS, Cascade's IP Navigator, as well as Cabletron's Secure Fast Virtual Networking.

At the Ingress LSR

Figure 3–4 shows how an ingress (edge) tag switching router (TSR) or a label switching router (LSR) processes an incoming IP datagram.[1] The incoming packet is stored in a queue to await processing. Once processing begins, the options field in the IP header is processed to determine if any options are in the header (the support for this operation

---

[1]TSR and LSR are different terms that describe the same kinds of operations. Some vendors use the term TSR and others use LSR. I will use LSR in this text, unless the specific explanations warrant the use of TSR.

varies; most routers can be configured to examine the type of service (TOS) bits). The datagram header is checked for any modifications that may have occurred during its journey to this IP node (with a checksum field). The destination IP address is examined. If the IP address is local, the IP PID field in the header is used to pass the data field to the next module, such as TCP, UDP, and ICMP.

If it is determined that the datagram is to be transported through an ATM or a Frame Relay network, the L_3 IP address in the destination field of the IP datagram is correlated to a tag or label that is stored in a table in the LSR. The datagram is then encapsulated into an ATM cell or a Frame Relay frame, with an encapsulation header attached to the datagram.

At an Intermediate (Interior) LSR

The traffic is sent to the outgoing interface for transport to the next node, where the ATM or Frame Relay VCID, or a label (and not the IP address), is examined to determine the actions to take on the data unit. This operation is shown in Figure 3–5. The label is examined to deter-

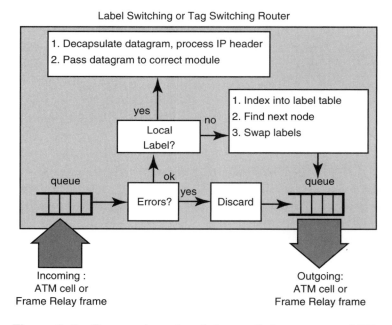

Figure 3–5   Processing at an intermediate or egress LSR.

mine if it is local or if it is a binding to the next node. If it is local, the packet is decapsulated and the IP header is used to process the traffic further. If the label indicates the packet is to be relayed to another node, the label is used to index into a label table to find how the packet is to be treated, including its priority, the next node (an egress interface), and the new label that is to replace the old label.

At the Egress LSR

Eventually, the packet will arrive at the final LSR. How the LSR determines that the protocol data unit is at the final node varies, but there must be some method to determine that the label is a local label that "belongs" to that local LSR. Through a process of local binding, which is an operation performed before the transmission of the user data occurs (and discussed later), the local LSR is able to access a table that identifies its labels on each incoming interface.

Therefore, when a cell or frame arrives, the LSR can quickly determine if the label is local; that is, if the traffic is to be terminated at this node and not passed through to the next node. This operation is also shown in Figure 3–5.

The process is straightforward. The ATM cell or Frame Relay header is processed, then removed. The encapsulation header is processed to determine the nature of the user's packet (for example, an IP datagram or an SNA message). Based on the values in the encapsulation header, the packet is passed to the proper module in the LSR or passed to a local machine (such as a router, server, or host) for further processing.

MPLS's Relationship to these Operations

The overall concepts of layer 3 to layer 2 mapping are found in other techniques, such as tag switching, Multiprotocol Over ATM (MPOA), and Multiprotocol Label Switching (MPLS). All of these systems perform some type of L_3 to L_2 mapping—they simply go about it in different ways.

IP SWITCHING

Several methods are employed to implement IP switching, and the term was coined by Ipsilon. For this discussion, we examine the use of a high-speed ATM switch, colocated with IP, and the approach used by Ipsilon (purchased by Nokia) and called IP switching.[2] Once again, it will be evident that many of the concepts explained here are present in other procedures in the taxonomy.

First, this approach uses the concept of a flow, which is a sequence of datagrams from one source machine or application to one or more machines or applications. For a long flow (many datagrams flowing between these entities), a router can cache information about the flow and circumvent the traditional IP routing mechanisms (subnet masking, search on longest subnet mask, and so on) by storing the routing information in cache, thus achieving high throughput.

Generally, the approach is to divert long flows, real-time traffic, or traffic with QOS requirements to an ATM connection, and use an individual ATM VPI/VCI for switching the traffic. For transaction-based traffic (database queries, such as a name server operation), the traffic is placed on a preassigned ATM virtual circuit.

One of the difficulties of managing an ATM virtual circuit (VC) is that its state (up, down, inactive, active, etc.) must be maintained end-to-end, with all switches on the VC keeping state information about the VC. If a failure occurs on any part of the VC, extensive signaling is required to clear the VC and take remedial action, such as setting up the VC again. However, if the signaling software is removed and replaced with software that keeps state information only on a local basis, the operations are much more efficient and correlate more closely to the IP's connectionless nature. The technique described here does not use end-to-end VCs; all are local to the two neighbor switches.

Architecture of the IP Switch

Figure 3–6 shows a simple view of the IP switch architecture. The switch contains the ATM switching fabric and IP switch controller, the General Switch Management Protocol (GSMP, see RFC 1987) and Ipsilon Flow Management Protocol (FMP, see RFC 1954).[3] The GSMP is used to provide the IP switch controller access to the ATM switching fabric. The FMP is used to associate IP flows with ATM VCs. The IP switch controller runs conventional IP routing and forwarding operations, in addition to GSM, FMP, and flow classification and control operations.

---

[2]For a more detailed description of this approach, see Newmand et. al., "IP Label Switching—ATM Under IP," IEEE/ACM *Transactions on Communications*, vol. 6, no. 2, April, 1998.

[3]Recent documents exclude Ipsilon's name from this protocol and use the initials FMP. I will follow this convention hereafter.

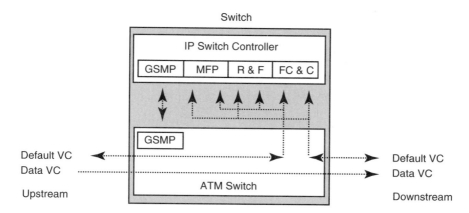

Figure 3–6   The IP switch architecture.

IP switching classifies a flow in two ways. The *host-pair flow* uses the source and destination IP addresses and time to live (TTL) to identify the flow. The *port-pair flow* identifies traffic flowing between the same source and destination ports, the same source and destination IP addresses, the same type of service (TOS), the same protocol ID (PID), and the same time to live (TTL). At first glance, one might question why all these fields are used. Why not just use the IP addresses? The answer is that identifying ports, protocols, and so on allows a switching decision to be made on the type of traffic—for example, a well known port such as file transfer or the Domain Name System (DNS). Thus, the file transfer traffic could be switched, and the DNS traffic could be routed. It makes little sense to build a VC for a one-time DNS query.

The host-pair flow is also called a type 2 flow. The *port-pair flow* is called a type 1 flow. So, the definition of a flow in IP switching depends on the type of flow, but includes a set of packets whose header fields are identical.

To get things started at system boot, a default VC is established between the switch (switch B) and all its neighbors (say, switches A and C). These VCs are used to forward IP datagrams on a hop-by-hop basis between switches. This VC is shown as the default VC in Figure 3–7 and is identified with a well known ATM VPI/VCI value. Since this default VC is provisioned as an ATM PVC (permanent virtual circuit), there is no requirement to use the ATM signaling protocol Q.2931. The default VC is also used to transfer packets that do not have a label associated with them. These packets are routed by the switch controller routing and forwarding module.

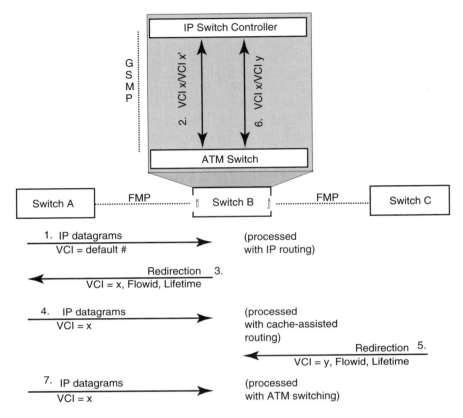

Figure 3–7   Flow redirection.

The FMP Operations. In Figure 3–7, we assume that datagrams arrive at switch A from switch B on the default VC at port i (event 1 in the figure). The IP switch controller (executing AAL5) reassembles the datagram and forwards it with conventional IP routing operations. We further assume that the IP switch controller decides that the datagrams belong to a new flow. In event 2, the controller selects an unused VCI label (say, x') to operate between the ATM switch and the controller at port c (this port is some type of association between the controller and the switch, and is not shown here). The controller selects an unused VCI (say, x) from a table associated with the input port (port i). Next, a switch driver is instructed to map VCI x on port i to VCI x' on port c. The value x' will be used as an index to cache has stored the relay information for this VC. The entry is created with GSMP.

In event 3, the switch controller sends an FMP message to the up-stream node that has been transmitting this flow. This message contains the label VC = x, a flow label, and a lifetime value. The flow label contains the header fields that set up the flow to begin with. The lifetime states how long the flow is valid.

For a brief period, the cells will arrive at port i with VCI = x, shown as event 4. These cells are mapped to VCI x', passed on port c to the controller, and forwarded to the next node. However, conventional routing table lookups are not performed because X' is used as an index into cache to obtain the forwarding information.

This intermediate step is needed until the next step occurs. Switch C has been receiving these datagrams and (in event 5) sends a redirection FMP message to its upstream neighbor (switch B) instructing it to redirect this flow to another VCI; in this example VCI = y. This redirect is on port j. Upon receiving this message, the controller instructs the driver to map x.i to y.j, shown as event 6. Thereafter, the traffic on this flow is no longer processed by the IP switch controller and conventional IP routing. Rather, the traffic is processed directly through the ATM switch to the output port, as depicted in event 7 in the figure.

ROUTE SERVER-BASED RELAYING

This approach is quite similar to the layer 3 to layer 2 address mapping. The main difference is that a designated machine performs route calculations in contrast to the layer 3 to layer 2 operation where the translation is performed in the same machine. Examples of this operation are MPOA and the Next Hop Resolution Protocol (NHRP). The route-server based operations still perform layer 3 to layer 2 address translations—it is simply done in a different machine (a server).

In Figure 3–8, a server residing in Network 1 is responsible for the support of the client's users' ability to reach destination nodes. The sources and sinks of the traffic are IP nodes, using conventional IP addresses, and the client might be a local router.

The client is not responsible for route discovery outside its routing domain to, say, network 2. This task is assumed by an egress router, running an external gateway protocol, such as the Border Gateway Protocol (BGP). The addresses discovered by the egress router are conveyed to the server.

Later, when user A sends traffic to user B, user A's datagram is intercepted by the client. The client's responsibility is to send this traffic to

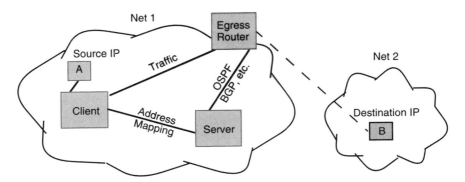

Figure 3–8   Route server-based relaying.

the most efficient egress point in the network. It may have this information stored locally. If not, it sends a request to the server.

The server knows about the destination IP address, courtesy of the egress router's keeping the server informed through the Open Shortest Path First, (OSPF), BGP, or some other routing protocol. The server will respond to the client's request by sending it a message containing the address of the egress router. The client then forwards this traffic for user B to the egress router, typically over an established ATM connection. The server could also send a label that is to be used for this particular flow.

Multiprotocol Over ATM (MPOA) and Next Hop Resolution Protocol (NHRP)

The principal objective of MPOA is to support the transfer of inter-subnet unicast traffic. MPOA allows the inter-subnetwork traffic based on layer 3 protocol communications to occur over ATM virtual channel connections (VCCs) without requiring routers in the data path. The goal of MPOA is to combine bridging and routing with ATM in a situation where diverse protocols and network topologies exist.

The job of MPOA is to provide this operation to allow the overlaying of layer 3 protocols (also called internetwork layer protocols) on ATM. MPOA is designed to use both routing and bridging information to locate the optimal route through the ATM backbone.

MPOA supports the concept of virtual routing, which is the separation of internetwork layer route calculation and forwarding. The idea behind virtual routing is to enhance the manageability of internetworking by decreasing the number of devices that are configured to perform route calculation. In so doing, virtual routing increases scalability by reducing the number of devices that participate in the internetwork layer route calculations.

MPOA is responsible for five major operations:

1. *Configuration.* This operation obtains configuration information from the emulated LAN configuration servers (ELAN LECS). These nodes are not important to this discussion; they contain timer information, requirements for the size of packets, etc.

2. *Discovery.* MPOA clients (MPCs) and MPOA servers (MPSs) dynamically learn of each others' existence. MPCs and MPSs discover each other by the exchange of messages. These messages carry the MPOA device type (MPC or MPS) and its ATM Address

3. *Target Resolution.* This operation uses a modified NHRP Resolution Request message to enable MPCs to find an appropriate ATM node to reach an IP destination (target) address. This ATM node is known as a shortcut to the destination.

4. *Connection Management.* This operation controls the ongoing management of ATM virtual circuits.

5. *Data Transfer.* This operation is responsible for forwarding of IP traffic across a shortcut.

MPOA incorporates the use of LANE and NHRP. Figure 3–9 is an example of the contents of the NHRP Request and Reply messages. The job of NHRP in this example is to map IP addresses to ATM addresses. To keep matters simple, we use the letters DEF and KLM to represent ATM addresses, which are based on the ITU-T Network Service Access Point (NSAP) standard.

We assume the client with addresses DEF/192.168.3.3 receives a datagram destined for station 192.168.2.3 that is located in NBMA 2.[4] Client DEF sends an NHRP request message to the server. Notice that the request message has the destination protocol address coded as the "target" protocol address of 192.168.2.3.

The NHS NHRP tables reveal that address 192.168.2 is reachable through KLM/192.168.3.2. Therefore, the server sends back the NHRP response message with the next hop fields coded to identify the egress router to NBMA 2. This router is identified with address KLM/192.168.3.2.

---

[4]NMBA are the initials for a nonbroadcast multiple access network, such as X.25 or Frame Relay, that is, a switched network.

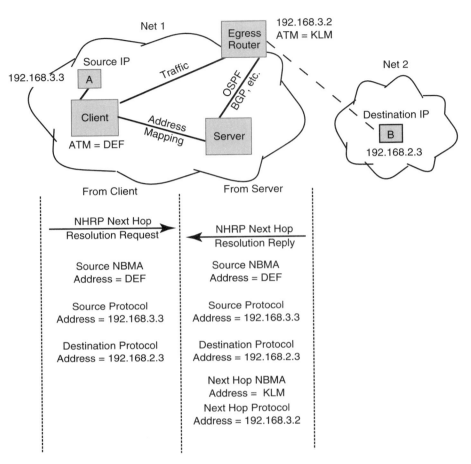

Figure 3–9   Example of NHRP operations.

TAG SWITCHING

As mentioned earlier, tag switching is a form of label switching. The concepts are based largely on Cisco's efforts. Tag switching is based on using a label (a tag) in place of an address for the relaying decision, and is published in RFC 2105. The ATM Forum's Multiprotocol Over ATM is one example of a tag switching specification. The efforts by Cisco have resulted in the Multiprotocol Label Switching (MPLS) group, which is working to publish a "vendor-neutral" label switching protocol. Many of the concepts explained in this part of the chapter are quite similar to

MPLS, and are implementations of many of the basic concepts introduced in Chapter 2.

Tag switching consists of two components: forwarding and control. The forwarding component uses the tag information (tags) carried by packets and the tag forwarding information maintained by a tag switch to perform packet forwarding. The control component is responsible for maintaining correct tag forwarding information among a group of interconnected tag switches.

Forwarding Component

The forwarding operation employed by tag switching is based on label swapping. When a packet with a tag is received by a tag switch, the switch uses the tag as an index in its tag information base (TIB). Each entry in the TIB consists of an incoming tag[5] and one or more subentries of the form (outgoing tag, outgoing interface, outgoing link information). If the switch finds an entry with the incoming tag equal to the tag carried in the packet, then it replaces the tag in the packet with the outgoing tag, if appropriate, and replaces the link information (e.g., MAC address) in the packet with the outgoing link-level information and forwards the packet over the outgoing interface.

The forwarding decision is based on the exact match algorithm using a fixed length short tag as an index. This enables a simplified forwarding procedure, in comparison to longest match forwarding traditionally used at the network layer. The forwarding procedure is simple enough to allow a hardware implementation.

The forwarding decision is independent of the tag's forwarding granularity. For example, the same forwarding algorithm applies to both unicast and multicast—a unicast entry would just have a single (outgoing tag, outgoing interface, outgoing link information) subentry, while a multicast entry may have one or more (outgoing tag, outgoing interface, outgoing link information) subentries. (For multiaccess links, the outgoing link-level information in this case would include a multicast MAC address.)

---

[5]Not stated in RFC 2105 is the possibility of associating the tag with its incoming interface, thus allowing the labels to be reused at each interface. This method allows the use of fewer bits for the label, instead of using a pool of labels for all the interfaces. Also, multicasting requires the association of the incoming datagram to the incoming interface. However, as noted later in this chapter, associating the tag with the incoming interface entails additional overhead.

The forwarding procedure is decoupled from the control component of tag switching. New routing (control) functions can be deployed without disturbing the forwarding operation.

Tag Encapsulation

Tag information can be carried in a packet in a variety of ways.

- As a small "shim" tag header inserted between the layer 2 and layer 3 headers
- As part of the layer 2 header, if the layer 2 header provides adequate semantics (e.g., ATM)
- As part of the header (e.g., using the flow label field in IPv6)

The tag forwarding component is L_3-independent. Use of control component(s) specific to a particular protocol enables the use of tag switching with different L_3 protocols.

Control Component

The control component is responsible for creating tag bindings and then distributing the tag binding information among tag switches. The control component is organized as a collection of modules, each designed to support a particular routing function. To support new routing functions, new modules can be added. The following describes some of the modules.

Destination-based Routing

To support destination-based routing with tag switching, a tag switch (just like a router) participates in the operations of the routing protocols (e.g., OSPF, BGP) and constructs its tag forwarding information base (TFIB) using the information it receives from these protocols.

There are three methods for tag allocation and TFIB management: (a) downstream tag allocation, (b) downstream tag allocation on demand, and (c) upstream tag allocation. In all three methods, a switch allocates tags and binds them to address prefixes in its TFIB.

In the downstream allocation, the tag that is carried in a packet is generated and bound to a prefix by the switch at the downstream end of the link (with respect to the direction of data flow). In the upstream allocation, tags are allocated and bound at the upstream end of the link. On demand allocation means that tags will only be allocated and distributed by the downstream switch when it is requested to do so by the upstream switch. The latter methods are most useful in ATM networks.

The downstream tag allocation scheme operates as follows: for each route in its TFIB, the switch allocates a tag, creates an entry in its TFIB with the incoming tag set to the allocated tag, and then advertises the binding between the (incoming) tag and the route to other adjacent tag switches. When a tag switch receives tag binding information for a route, and that information was originated by the next hop for that route, the switch places the tag (carried as part of the binding information) into the outgoing tag of the TFIB entry associated with the route. This creates the binding between the outgoing tag and the route.

With the downstream tag allocation on demand scheme, for each route in its TFIB, the switch identifies the next hop for that route. It then issues a request via a Tag Distribution Protocol (TDP) to the next hop for a tag binding for that route. When the next hop receives the request, it allocates a tag, creates an entry in its TFIB with the incoming tag set to the allocated tag, and then returns the binding between the (incoming) tag and the route to the switch that sent the original request. When the switch receives the binding information, the switch creates an entry in its TFIB and sets the outgoing tag in the entry to the value received from the next hop.

The upstream tag allocation scheme is used as follows. If a tag switch has one or more point-to-point interfaces, then for each route in its TFIB whose next hop is reachable via one of these interfaces, the switch allocates a tag, creates an entry in its TFIB with the outgoing tag set to the allocated tag, and then advertises to the next hop (via TDP) the binding between the (outgoing) tag and the route. When a tag switch that is the next hop receives the tag binding information, the switch places the tag (carried as part of the binding information) into the incoming tag of the TFIB entry associated with the route.

Once a TFIB entry is populated with both incoming and outgoing tags, the tag switch can forward packets for routes bound to the tags by using the tag switching forwarding algorithm.

When a tag switch creates a binding between an outgoing tag and a route, the switch updates its TFIB with the binding information.

A tag switch will try to populate its TFIB with incoming and outgoing tags for all routes to which it has reachability, so that all packets can be forwarded by simple label swapping. Tag allocation is thus driven by topology (routing), not traffic—it is the existence of a TFIB entry that causes tag allocations, not the arrival of data packets.

Use of tags associated with routes, rather than flows, also means that there is no need to perform flow classification procedures for all the flows to determine whether to assign a tag to a flow.

Multicast and Tag Switching

Essential to multicast routing is the notion of spanning trees. Multicast routing procedures are responsible for constructing such trees (with receivers as leafs), while multicast forwarding is responsible for forwarding multicast packets along such trees.

To support a multicast forwarding function with tag switching, each tag switch associates a tag with a multicast tree as follows. When a tag switch creates a multicast forwarding entry (either for a shared or for a source-specific tree), and the list of outgoing interfaces for the entry, the switch also creates local tags (one per outgoing interface). The switch creates an entry in its TFIB and populates (outgoing tag, outgoing interface, outgoing MAC header) with this information for each outgoing interface, placing a locally generated tag in the outgoing tag field. This creates a binding between a multicast tree and the tags. The switch then advertises over each outgoing interface associated with the entry the binding between the tag (associated with this interface) and the tree.

When a tag switch receives a binding between a multicast tree and a tag from another tag switch, if the other switch is the upstream neighbor (with respect to the multicast tree), the local switch places the tag carried in the binding into the incoming tag component of the TFIB entry associated with the tree.

When a set of tag switches are interconnected via a multiple-access subnetwork, the tag allocation procedure for multicast has to be coordinated among the switches. In all other cases, tag allocation procedure for multicast could be the same as for tags used with destination-based routing.

Flexible Routing (Explicit Routes)

One of the properties of destination-based routing is that the only information from a packet that is used to forward the packet is the destination address. While this property enables scaleable routing, it also limits the ability to influence the actual paths taken by packets. This, in turn, limits the ability to evenly distribute traffic among multiple links, taking the load off highly utilized links and shifting it towards less utilized links. For Internet Service Providers (ISPs) who support different classes of service, destination-based routing also limits their ability to segregate different classes with respect to the links used by these classes. Some of the ISPs today use Frame Relay or ATM to overcome the limitations imposed by destination-based routing. Tag switching, because of the flexible granularity of tags, is able to overcome these limitations without using either Frame Relay or ATM.

To provide forwarding along the paths that are different from the paths determined by the destination-based routing, the control component of tag switching allows installation of tag bindings in tag switches that do not correspond to the destination-based routing paths. Of course, this idea is also fundamental to MPLS.

Tag Switching with ATM

Since tag switching is based on label swapping, and since ATM forwarding is also based on label swapping, tag switching technology can readily be applied to ATM switches by implementing the control component of tag switching.

The tag information needed for tag switching can be carried in the VCI field. If two levels of tagging are needed, then the VPI field could be used as well, although the size of the VPI field limits the size of networks in which this would be practical.[6] However, for most applications of one level of tagging, the VCI field is adequate.

To obtain the necessary control information, the switch should be able to participate as a peer in L_3 routing protocols (e.g., OSPF, BGP). If the switch has to perform routing information aggregation, then to support destination-based unicast routing, the switch should be able to perform L_3 forwarding for some fraction of the traffic as well.

Supporting the destination-based routing function with tag switching on an ATM switch may require the switch to maintain not one, but several tags associated with a route (or a group of routes with the same next hop). This is necessary to avoid the interleaving of packets that arrive from different upstream tag switches, but are sent concurrently to the same next hop. Either the downstream tag allocation on demand or the upstream tag allocation scheme could be used for the tag allocation and TFIB maintenance procedures with ATM switches.

Therefore, an ATM switch can support tag switching, but at the minimum, it needs to implement L_3 routing protocols and the tag

---

[6]This statement from RFC 2105 is open to question. If the VPI label is terminated at each interface, its size should not present a problem.

switching control component on the switch. It may also need to support some network layer forwarding.

Implementing tag switching on an ATM switch simplifies integration of ATM switches and routers—an ATM switch capable of tag switching appears as a router to an adjacent router.

Quality of Service

Two mechanisms are needed for providing QOS to packets passing through a router or a tag switch. First, packets are identified as different classes. Second, appropriate QOS (bandwidth, loss, etc.) is provided to each class.

Tag switching provides an easy way to mark packets as belonging to a particular class after they have been classified the first time. Initial classification would be done using information carried in the L_3 layer or higher layer headers, a concept explained in this book as an FEC. A tag corresponding to the resultant class would then be applied to the packet. Tagged packets can then be handled by the tag switching routers in their paths without needing to be reclassified.

Examples of Tag Switching Operations

This section should piece together many of the concepts just discussed. Figure 3–10 is used as an initial example for this discussion. We use generic addresses in this example for simplicity. Addresses XYZ and HIJ can be IP, IPX, ATM, AppleTalk addresses, and so on. Most likely, they are subnet or aggregated addresses with address prefixes.

The TSRs perform local binding (LB) of tags to interfaces. For example, TSR A has stored in its TFIB a binding of tag 21 to interface b. The other TSRs have stored bindings as follows:

TSR B   30.a
TSR C   21.d
TSR D   14.b

Through ongoing link-state route advertising (such as OSPF), routing information is flooded to the TSRs. Let us assume packets will be sent to address HIJ, so OSPF is used to build forwarding tables in each TSR to enable the TSR to forward traffic to a next hop to reach HIJ.

Upon, say, TSR B finding a router (a next hop) to HIJ, it selects a tag from a pool of free tags. It uses the tag to index into its TFIB and up-

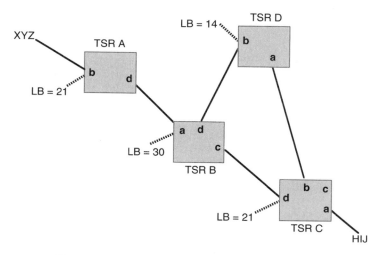

Figure 3–10 Tag switching routes (TSRs).

dates this entry with (a) incoming tag of 30, (b) the associated incoming interface of a, (c) the address of the next hop, and (d) the outgoing interface to that next hop.

An important note: Our description of this operation assumes that TSR B knows the incoming interface of 30 in relation to a binding between XYZ and HIJ. Well, it may not. If the OSPF information came from (downstream) TSR C, TSR B cannot know the upstream interface until it *actually* receives a datagram destined for HIJ on interface a. This approach of associating tags with outgoing *and* incoming interfaces requires extra bookkeeping and more steps in binding the two tags/interfaces together. A viable alternative is to not associate a tag with an incoming interface, which means the tag pool is for all interfaces. This approach works if the length (in bits) of the tag is sufficient for all interfaces. Anyway, it requires some thought and I have shown the TFIBs in Table 3–1 and Table 3–2 both ways: with and without an association to the incoming interface. Be aware that the Cisco tag switching specification does not populate the incoming interface.

The results of the TFIB updates are shown in Table 3–1. Notice that the outgoing tag in the TFIB is not yet populated. Thus far, the local binding operations have only created information on incoming tags. The outgoing tags are populated by the TSRs distributing their local binding information, which is discussed next.

Table 3–1(a)   TFIB: Initial Population with Correlation to Incoming Interface

TSR	Incoming Tag	Incoming Interface	Outgoing Tag	Outgoing Interface	Next Hop to HIJ
A	21	b	—	d	TSR B
B	30	a	—	c	TSR C
C	21	d	—	a	HIJ (DIR)
D	14	b	—	a	TSR C

(Note: Row entries reflect an entry at each TSR.)

Table 3–1(b)   TFIB: Initial Population with No Correlation to Incoming Interface

TSR	Incoming Tag	Outgoing Tag	Outgoing Interface	Next Hop to HIJ
A	21	—	d	TSR B
B	30	—	c	TSR C
C	21	—	a	HIJ (DIR)
D	14	—	a	TSR C

(Note: Row entries reflect an entry at each TSR.)

In Figure 3–11, TSR B distributes its local binding information to all TSRs in the routing domain (TSRs C and D). Both TSR C and D ignore this information *because* TSR B is not the next hop to HIJ.

In Figure 3–12, TSR B receives the binding information from TSR C and TSR D. It ignores the information for TSR D because this node is not

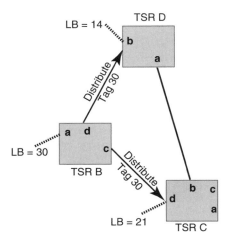

Figure 3–11   Tag information distribution.

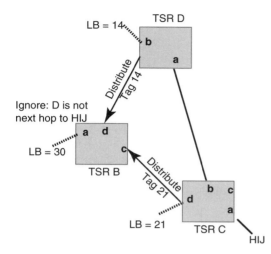

Figure 3–12   A remote binding.

the next hop to HIJ. It accepts the information for TSR C because C is the next hop to HIJ. This remote binding information is used to populate TSR B's TFIB, by using the tag of 21 from TSR C's message.

Eventually, the TFIBs are fully populated, as shown in Table 3–2.

Table 3–2(a)   TFIB: Final Population with Correlation to Incoming Interface.

TSR	Incoming Tag	Incoming Interface	Outgoing Tag	Outgoing Interface	Next Hop to HIJ
A	21	b	30	d	TSR B
B	30	a	21	c	TSR C
C	21	d	—	a	HIJ (DIR)
D	14	b	17	a	TSR C

(Note: Row entries reflect an entry at each TSR.)

Table 3–2(b)   TFIB: Final Population with no Correlation to Incoming Interface

TSR	Incoming Tag	Outgoing Tag	Outgoing Interface	Next Hop to HIJ
A	21	30	d	TSR B
B	30	21	c	TSR C
C	21	—	a	HIJ (DIR)
D	14	17	a	TSR C

(Note: Row entries reflect an entry at each TSR.)

Border (Edge) TSRs

Tag switching is designed to scale to large networks. Its scaling capability is based on its ability to carry more than one tag in the packet. As we will see, *tag stacking* allows designated TSRs to exchange information with each other and act as border nodes to a large domain of networks and other TSRs. These other TSRs are *interior* nodes to the domain and do not concern themselves with interdomain routes, a concept also found in MPLS.

We will modify Figure 3–10 to Figure 3–13 in this discussion. Assume that three TSRs are members of the same domain (domain B) and TSR A and TSR C are border TSRs. This example will also assume that this domain is a transit domain (in which the packets traversing it neither originate nor terminate in this domain). It is certainly desirable to isolate the intradomain TSRs from these operations. In fact, we will show that the interior TSRs need to store in their TFIBs only the routing information to reach their correct border router.

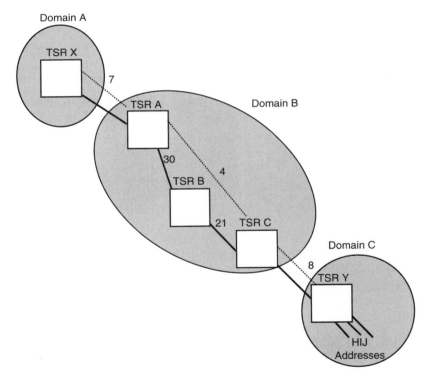

Figure 3–13   **Border TSRs and domains.**

Border TSR X and TSR Y are the designated border routers for domains A and C, respectively. To advertise addresses from, say, domain C, TSR Y distributes information to TSR C, which distributes it to TSR A, which then distributes it to TSR X. It is not distributed to TSR B because TSR B is an interior TSR.

We will dispense with the interface entries in Table 3–3, which shows the TFIB from domain B.

Assume the following: (a) TSR Y creates a local binding for the HIJ addresses in domain C using 8 as the local tag; (b) TSR C creates a local binding for the same HIJ addresses using 4 as the local tag; (c) TSR A does the same with a local tag of 7.

Using the tag distribution procedures discussed earlier, the following events occur: (a) TSR Y distributes its tag 8 to TSR C, which uses it as an outgoing tag to the HIJ addresses; (b) TSR C distributes its tag 4 to TSR A, which uses it as an outgoing tag to the HIJ addresses; and (c) TSR A distributes its tag 7 to TSR X.

In addition, when TSR A receives the tag binding message from next hop border TSR C, it notes that TSR C is not connected directly to TSR A. It must store this information and use it later for ongoing packet transfer, discussed next.

Now, assume that a packet destined for one of the addresses in the aggregate HIJ address arrives at TSR X. TSR X sends this packet to TSR A with tag = 7. At TSR A, tag 7 is swapped for tag 4. Also, TSR A knows that this tag pertains to border TSR C, which is not connected directly to TSR A. In order to route the packet, TSR A pushes tag 30 onto the tag stack in the packet.

Therefore, the packet will contain two tags when transiting this routing domain. This approach keeps the internal TSRs isolated from interdomain routing.

To continue this example, TSR A sends the packet to TSR B, and TSR B swaps tag 30 for tag 21, then sends the packet to TSR C. TSR C's analysis of tag 21 must reveal that TSR C is to pop the tag stack in the packet, where tag 4 is found (placed there by border TSR A). TSR C then

Table 3–3   TFIB for Domain B

TSR	IncomingTag	OutgoingTag	Next Hop
A	—	30	B
B	30	21	C
C	21	—	—

swaps tag 4 with tag 8 and sends the packet to TSR 2 and domain C, where address HIJ can be found.

Flow Classification

This book has made several comments on flow classification. It plays a role in all label switching networks. I include it in our taxonomy to make certain its importance is recognized. Recall that a flow is a sequence of user packets from one source machine and application to one or more machines and applications. A router can cache information about the flow and circumvent the traditional IP routing mechanisms (subnet masking, search on longest subnet mask, and so on) by storing the routing information in cache, thus achieving high throughput and low delay. The flow is usually associated with an FEC, a topic explained in Chapter 2.

IPv6 Flow Operations

The IPv6 header contains a flow label field. When IPv6 is eventually implemented, this field will likely be used to support FEC and label switching operations. Figure 3–14 illustrates the format of IPv6 datagram (also called a packet, in some literature).

The *flow label* field is designed to handle different types of traffic, such as voice, video, or data. The flow label field is a special identifier that can be attached to the datagram to permit it to be given special treatment by a router. It is called the flow label field because its intent is to identify traffic in which multiple datagrams are "flowing" from a specific source address to a specific destination address. The use of the flow label field can be used in place of the IP destination address fields, but its specific use is implementation-specific. Section 6 of RFC 1883 provides guidance on the use of flow labels.

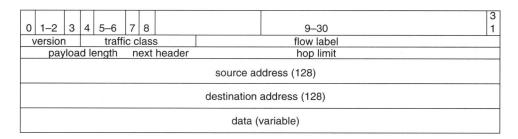

Figure 3–14   The IPv6 datagram.

IPV4 CODEPOINT OPERATIONS

A recent revision to the IP TOS field has been made to support differentiated services (DS), a topic covered in Chapter 8. It is called the DS codepoint (DSCP). The DS codepoint is explained in considerable detail in Chapter 8.

MPLS AND LDP

MPLS is the Internet standard for label switching. The idea of MPLS is to use an operation at the edge of the network to assign labels to each packet. These labels, in turn, are used to route the traffic from the source to the destination. Since this book concentrates on MPLS and LDP, further discussions on this part of the taxonomy are deferred to later chapters.

IPv6 Label Operations

This operation uses the IPv6 flow label field in the header. I place this category separately from the IPv6 Flow category because the label need not be associated with a flow (but in practice, it probably will be).

SUMMARY

It is obvious from reading this chapter that the various concepts of label switching and forwarding have many overlapping characteristics. Indeed, some of them are more similar to each other than they are different. Nonetheless, each one has its own personality and each one has different backers in the industry. How each of these technologies will fare in the market has yet to be decided. However, as of this writing, ATM-based label switching has been widely deployed, and work is nearly complete on MPLS and supporting protocols, the subject of the next chapters.

4

MPLS Key Concepts

T his chapter examines the Multiprotocol Label Switching (MPLS) architecture, based on [ROSE00].[1] The major features of MPLS are explained with emphasis on the operations of LSRs and label assignments, swapping, merging, and aggregation. Label switching path (LSP) tunnels are investigated, along with label stacks and label hierarchies.

Label distribution protocols (LDPs) are responsible for the distribution of labels. Some general comments are made in this chapter about this subject, with Chapter 5 devoted to label distribution.

MAJOR ATTRIBUTES OF MPLS

Let's begin by describing some of the major attributes of MPLS, with a summary in Table 4–1. First, MPLS supports the concepts of streams (flows) and labels. The labels are not mapped end-to-end, but are managed locally between neighboring label switching routers (LSRs). Alternately, they may be passed through an LSR, unexamined, to other routers on the LSP.

---

[1][ROSE00] Rosen, Eric C. et. al., "Multiprotocol Label Switching Architecture," *draft-ietf-mpls-07.txt*, July 2000.

Table 4–1   Major Attributes of MPLS

- Streams and labels
- Can use various L_2 networks
- Supports source (explicit) routing
- Compatible with OSPF and BGP
- Labels are local
- Uses edge device concept
- QOS can be inferred from label

MPLS may or may not use an underlying backbone technology, such as Frame Relay or ATM, and the specifications do not restrict an MPLS network in this regard. In fact, the MPLS label can reside in the DLCI or VPI/VCI fields of the Frame Relay or ATM headers respectively.

MPLS supports the concepts of source (or explicit) routing, wherein the originator of the traffic can dictate the route through a routing domain. However, unlike conventional source routing protocols, it is not necessary to carry the route in each protocol data unit, such as the source routing option in IP. The label can be used to represent the route. MPLS does not replace, and indeed is compatible with, OSPF and BGP. Also, MPLS uses the edge device concept, wherein much of the work and processing overhead is performed before the traffic enters a core network.

MPLS eliminates the need to use the Next Hop Resolution Protocol (NHRP) and cut through SVCs (discussed in Chapter 3), which in turn eliminates the latency associated with these operations.

The assignment of a packet to an FEC is done once, at the edge LSR, which is associated with a label. Afterwards, there is no further examination of the IP header. Instead, the label is used as an index into a table, which specifies the new label and the next hop for the packet.

In addition, the QOS operations performed on the packet can be (but not required to be) inferred from the label itself. So, the label can represent the FEC and the QOS associated with the packet.

TERMINOLOGY

In addition to the terms explained in the last three chapters, these terms are used hereafter in this book.

- *Label merging.* The replacement of multiple incoming labels for a particular FEC with a single outgoing label.

- *Label switched hop.* The hop between two MPLS nodes on which forwarding is done using labels.
- *Label switched path.* The path through one or more LSRs, followed by packets in a particular FEC.
- *Label stack.* An ordered set of labels.
- *Merge point.* A node at which label merging is done.
- *Switched path.* Synonymous with label switched path.
- *VC merge.* Label merging in which the MPLS label is carried in the ATM VCI or combined VCI/VPI fields.
- *VP merge.* Label merging in which the MPLS label is carried in the ATM VPI field. The same VCI in two cells indicates the cells originated from the same node.

LABEL ASSIGNMENT RULES

MPLS defines the procedures to bind a label (say, label L) to an FEC (say, FEC F). The binding decision can be made by the downstream LSR. The downstream LSR then informs the upstream LSR about the binding. Thus, according to our definitions discussed earlier, MPLS labels can be downstream-assigned, with the label bindings distributed from the downstream LSR to the upstream LSR.

MPLS allows some variations to the downstream binding. One operation, called *downstream-on-demand* label distribution allows an LSR to request from its next hop LSR a label binding for a particular FEC.

The first option, wherein the downstream LSR distributes bindings to LSRs that have not requested them, is called *unsolicited downstream* label distribution.

TYPES OF MPLS NODES

Figure 4–1 shows the three types of MPLS nodes. They perform the following functions:

- *Ingress LSR.* Receives native-mode user traffic (for example, IP datagrams) and classifies it into an FEC. It then generates an MPLS header and assigns it a label. The IP datagram is encapsulated into the MPLS PDU, with the MPLS header attached to the datagram. If it is integrated with a QOS operation (say, DiffServ),

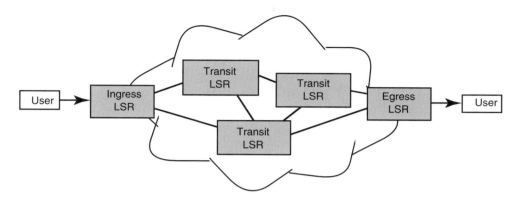

Figure 4–1   The MPLS nodes.

the ingress LSR will condition the traffic in accordance with the DiffServ rules.

- *Transit LSR.* Receives the PDU and uses the MPLS header to make forwarding decisions. It will also perform label swapping. It is not concerned with processing the L_3 header, only the label header. Some papers call this LSR an *interior LSR.*
- *Egress LSR.* Performs the decapsulation operations, in that it removes the MPLS header.

In Figure 4–2, nodes A, B, G, and H are user machines and are not configured with MPLS. Node C is the ingress LSR, nodes D and E are transit LSRs, and node F is the egress LSR. This figure uses generic addresses. For example, the address for node G is "G," which could be an IP address or some other address, such as IPX or a telephone number.

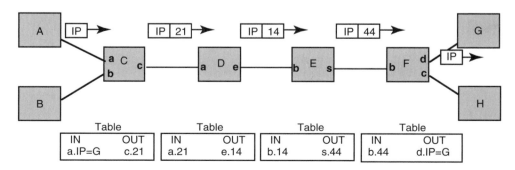

Figure 4–2   Label swapping and forwarding.

LSR C receives an IP datagram from user node A on interface a. This datagram is destined for node G. LSR C analyzes the FEC fields, correlates the FEC with label 21, encapsulates the datagram behind a label header, and sends the packet to output interface c. The OUT entry in LSR C's table directs it to place label 21 onto the label header in the packet. This operation at LSR C is called a *label push,* and is explained shortly.

Hereafter, LSRs D and E process only the label header, and their swapping tables are used (at LSR D) to swap label 21 for label 14, and (at LSR E) to swap label 14 for label 44. Notice that the swapping tables use the ingress and egress interfaces at each LSR to correlate the labels to the ingress and egress communications links. Egress LSR F is configured to recognize label 44 on interface b as its own label; that is, there are no more hops. Notice the OUT entry in F's table directs LSR F to send this datagram to G on interface d; this implies removing the label from the packet. This label removal is part of an operation called a *label pop,* and is explained shortly.

INDEPENDENT AND ORDERED LABEL CONTROL

MPLS supports two methods of label assignment to an FEC. The first is called *independent control* and is shown in Figure 4–3. LSR A has used OSPF to advertise address prefix 192.168/19 to LSR B in event 1. Upon receiving this advertisement, LSR B independently assigns a label to this FEC and advertises this label assignment to its neighbors, LSR A and LSR C in events 2 and 2a. The notations 2 and 2a are meant to convey that the order in which these label assignments are sent will vary, based on some rules explained later in this chapter.

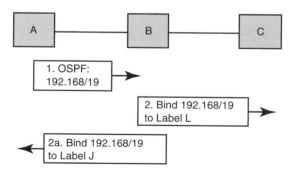

Figure 4–3   Independent control.

The advantage to independent control is that the label assignment operations occur just after the advertising of the address. Assuming the address advertisement leads to rapid routing convergence (the routing tables in the routing domain are stable and are in sync with each other), the associated labels are set up quite quickly, thus allowing the network to use the more efficient labels in a timely fashion. However, independent control should be set up so that neighbor LSRs are in agreement on the FECs (address prefixes) they will use. If the decisions are different on the FECs, some FECs may not have LSPs associated with them, or they could be set up inefficiently. For example, in Figure 4–3, say, LSRs B and C may make different choices about FECs. Only LSR B is depicted in this example doing its independent operation, but LSR C could be doing its own binding assignments as well, so the assignments might not be consistent.

The second method is *ordered control,* shown in Figure 4–4. It is so named because the label assignments occur in an ordered manner, either from the ingress or egress LSR of an LSP. The example in Figure 4–4 shows the operation emanating from the egress LSR C (it knows it is the egress for the address prefix (the FEC) if the next hop for the address is not a neighbor LSR).

Unlike independent control, ordered control assures that all LSRs use the same FEC as the initial advertiser, LSR C in the example. This alternative also allows a network administrator some leeway in controlling how LSPs are established. For example, at the egress LSR, lists can be configured that instruct the LSR as to which FECs are to be correlated with an LSP, and thus subject to label switching.

The downside to ordered control is that it takes more time than independent control to establish the LSP. Some people consider this latency a

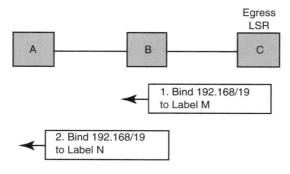

Figure 4–4   Ordered control.

small price to pay for the control it gives the network administrator. Others think ordered control is too cumbersome. For MPLS, both approaches are supported, but keep in mind that ordered control should be implemented at all LSRs if it is going to be effective. We will return to the subject of ordered control in Chapter 9, dealing with constraint-based routing.

THE MPLS HEADER

MPLS defines a header. It is 32 bits long and is created at the ingress LSR. It must reside behind any L_2 headers and in front of an L_3 header (in the example in Figure 4–5 IP). As discussed earlier, the IP (and maybe the L_4 header) is used by the ingress LSR to ascertain an FEC, which in turn is used to create the label. Thereafter, and once again, the label only is processed by the transit LSRs.

The format for the MPLS header is shown in Figure 4–6. It consists of the following fields:

- *Label.* Label value, 20 bits. This value contains the MPLS label.
- *Exp.* Experimental use, 3 bits. This field is not yet fully defined. Several Internet working papers on DiffServ discuss its use with this specification.
- *S.* Stacking bit, 1 bit. Used to stack multiple labels, and discussed later in this chapter.
- *TTL.* Time to live, 8 bits. Places a limit on how many hops the MPLS packet can traverse. This is needed because the IP TTL field is not examined by the transit LSRs.

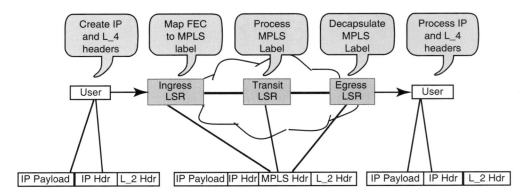

Figure 4–5   Creating and processing the MPLS header.

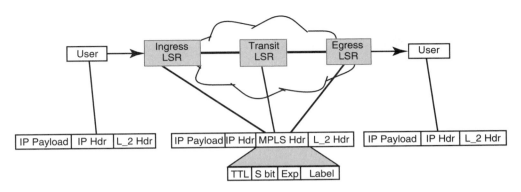

Figure 4–6   Format of the header.

THE LABEL STACK

Label switching is designed to scale to large networks, and MPLS supports label switching with hierarchical operations, which is based on the ability of MPLS to carry more than one label in the packet. Label stacking allows designated LSRs to exchange information with each other and act as border nodes to a large domain of networks and other LSRs. Recall that these other LSRs are interior nodes (transit nodes) to the domain and do not concern themselves with interdomain routes, nor with the labels associated with these routes.

The processing of a labeled packet is completely independent of the level of hierarchy; that is, the level of the label is not relevant to the LSR. To keep the operations simple, the processing is always based on the top label, without regard to the possibility that some number of other labels may have been above it in the past, or that some number of other labels may be below it at present. In Figure 4–2, the label stack was 1 as the packet was sent from C to D to E to F. An unlabeled packet can be thought of as a packet whose label stack is empty (i.e., whose label stack has depth 0). In Figure 4–2, the path from A to C, and from F to G, had an empty label stack, of course.

If a packet's label stack is of depth m, the label at the bottom of the stack is the level 1 label, to the label above it (if such exists) as the level 2 label, and to the label at the top of the stack as the level m label.

In Figure 4–7, assume that three LSRs are members of the same domain (domain B) and LSR A and LSR C are border LSRs. This example will also assume that this domain is a transit domain (in which the packets traversing it neither originate nor terminate in this domain). It is certainly desirable to isolate the intradomain LSRs from these operations.

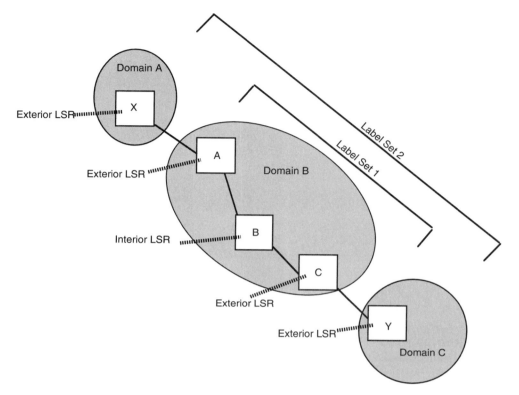

Figure 4–7   Label stacks and hierarchies.

LSR X and LSR Y are the designated border routers for domains A and C, respectively. To advertise addresses from, say, domain C, LSR Y distributes information to LSR C, which distributes it to LSR A, which then distributes it to LSR X. It is not distributed to LSR B because LSR B is an interior LSR.

Two levels of labels are used, as are two types of routing protocols. MPLS is used with OSPF in domain B, and BGP is used between domains A and B, and domains B and C. When traffic traverses through domain B, one level of labels is used, and the labels pertaining to the interdomain operations are pushed down in a label stack in the packet.

Figure 4–8 shows examples of label stacks. Nodes A, B, G, and H are exterior nodes (ingress and egress LSRs) to the internal domain where nodes C, D, E, and F reside. The LSR tables at nodes C and F have label stacks of a depth of 2. LSR D and LSR E tables have label stacks of a depth of 1. Notice that this example is slightly different from Figure 4–2.

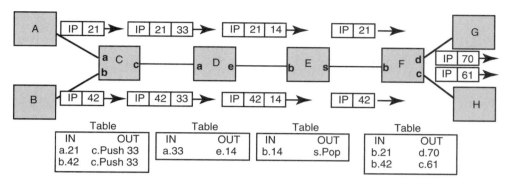

Figure 4–8   Example of label stacking: LSR E pops the stack.

In this example, we have extended the MPLS capabilities out to nodes A, B, G, and H. Therefore, sitting behind these nodes are most likely some non-MPLS nodes, such as workstations and servers.

Node A sends a packet to node C with a label of 21. Node C consults its label table and determines that the label is to be pushed down and label 33 used between node C and node D. The packet sent to node D has two labels, but label 21 is not examined by node D. Its label table directs it to swap label 33 for 14 and relay the packet out of interface e, a link to node E.

Upon node E receiving this packet, its label table instructs it to pop up the next label and then make a mapping to interface S. There is now only one label in the header. At node F, the label value of 21 on interface b is correlated to label 70 on interface d, the link to node G.

The second example in the figure is a packet emanating from node B, with a label value of 42. The label table at node C indicates this label is to be pushed, and label 33 is used as the outer label. The process then proceeds in the same manner as the first example until the traffic reaches node F. Here, the pop up operation reveals label 42, which is correlated with label 61 on interface c, the link to node H.

In this example, only one label binding was needed at the interior LSRs to handle two external labels. Of course, it is possible to map thousands of labels from exterior nodes to one label binding in an interior domain.

Figure 4–9 shows another example. In this operation, LSR F pops the stack and LSR E does not. LSR E processes the outer label just as LSR D has done.

Figure 4–10 shows one more example of label stacking. In this situation, nodes G and H are not LSRs. They are end stations, such as servers

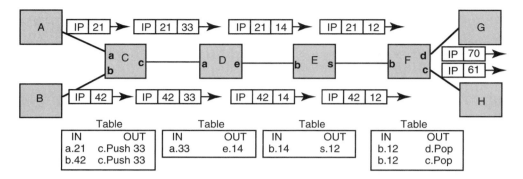

Figure 4–9   Example of label stacking: LSR F pops the stack.

or routers, that are not configured for MPLS operations. Two label pops occur, the first at LSR E and the second at LSR F. These three scenarios in Figures 4–8, 4–9, and 4–10 are all permitted, and the reasons for these choices are explained shortly.

RULES FOR STACKING FOR THE LABEL SWITCHED PATH

The explanation on the next page explains the rules for the label stacks, as provided in section 3.15 of the MPLS working draft [ROSE00]. In summary, these rules ensure that when an LSR pushes a label onto a packet that is already labeled, the new label corresponds to an FEC whose LSP egress is the LSR that assigned the label that is now second in the stack.

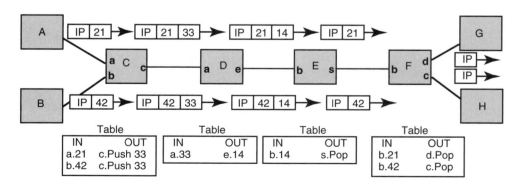

Figure 4–10   Two label pops.

A "Label Switched Path (LSP) of level m" for a particular
packet P is a sequence of routers,
<R1, ..., Rn>
with the following properties:

1. R1, the "LSP Ingress", is an LSR which pushes a label
   onto P's label stack, resulting in a label stack of
   depth m;
2. For all i, 1<i<n, P has a label stack of depth m when
   received by LSR Ri;
3. At no time during P's transit from R1 to R[n-1] does its
   labelstack ever have a depth of less than m;
4. For all i, 1<i<n: Ri transmits P to R[i+1] by means of
   MPLS, i.e., by using the label at the top of the label
   stack (the level m label) as an index into an incoming
   label map (ILM);
5. For all i, 1<i<n: if a system S receives and forwards P
   after P is transmitted by Ri but before P is received by
   R[i+1] (e.g., Ri and R[i+1] might be connected via a
   switched data link subnetwork, and S might be one of the
   data link switches), then S's forwarding decision is not
   based on the level m label, or on the network layer
   header. This may be because:

- the decision is not based on the label stack or the network layer;
- the decision is based on a label stack on which additional labels have been pushed (i.e., on a level m+k
  label, where k>0).

Penultimate Hop Popping

In Figure 4–10, a label pop is performed by LSR E and the other by
LSR F. One might wonder why the stacking did not continue to LSR F.
The answer is that it can indeed be extended to LSR F. The decision as to
where the final pop occurs is based on (a) the capability of the LSR, and
(b) the possible desire to execute no more than one label pop at each LSR.
Let's pick up on the MPLS specification here (a direct quote) to help understand these statements [ROSE00], section 3.16:

If <R1, ..., Rn> is a level m LSP for packet P, P may be
transmitted from R[n-1] to Rn with a label stack of depth
m-1. That is, the label stack may be popped at the penultimate LSR of the LSP, rather than at the LSP egress.

From an architectural perspective, this is perfectly appropriate. The purpose of the level m label is to get the packet to Rn. Once R[n-1] has decided to send the packet to Rn, the label no longer has any function, and need no longer be carried.

There is also a practical advantage to doing penultimate hop popping. It first looks up the top label, and determines as a result of that lookup that it is indeed the LSP egress. Then it must pop the stack, and examine what remains of the packet. If there is another label on the stack, the egress will look this up and forward the packet based on this lookup. (In this case, the egress for the packet's level m LSP is also an intermediate node for its level m-1 LSP.) If there is no other label on the stack, then the packet is forwarded according to its network layer destination address. Note that this would require the egress to do TWO lookups, either two label lookups or a label lookup followed by an address lookup.

This technique allows the egress to do a single lookup, and also requires only a single lookup by the penultimate node.

The creation of the forwarding "fastpath" in a label switching product may be greatly aided if it is known that only a single lookup is ever required:

- the code may be simplified if it can assume that only a single lookup is ever needed
- the code can be based on a "time budget" that assumes that only a single lookup is ever needed.

In fact, when penultimate hop popping is done, the LSP Egress need not even be an LSR.

However, some hardware switching engines may not be able to pop the label stack, so this cannot be universally required. There may also be some situations in which penultimate hop popping is not desirable. Therefore the penultimate node pops the label stack only if this is specifically requested by the egress node, OR if the next node in the LSP does not support MPLS. (If the next node in the LSP does support MPLS, but does not make such a request, the penultimate node has no way of knowing that it in fact is the penultimate node.)

An LSR which is capable of popping the label stack at all MUST do penultimate hop popping when so requested by its downstream label distribution peer.

Stacks and Encapsulations

The procedures for identifying the label stack and encapsulating it in lower layer protocols, such as PPP or ATM, are specified in [ROSE99a].[2] The format for the label stack was introduced in Figure 4–6

The label stack entries appear after the data link layer headers, but before any network layer headers. The top of the label stack appears earliest in the packet, and the bottom appears latest. The network layer packet immediately follows the label stack entry that has the S bit set.

When a labeled packet is received, the label value at the top of the stack is looked up. As a result of a successful lookup, the LSR knows the next hop for the packet and the operation that is to be performed on the packet, such as pushing or popping operations.

Reserved Label Values.   Several label values are reserved. They are as follows:

- A value of 0 represents the "IPv4 Explicit NULL Label." This label value is only legal when it is the sole label stack entry. It indicates that the label stack must be popped, and the forwarding of the packet must then be based on the IPv4 header.
- A value of 1 represents the "Router Alert Label." This label value is legal anywhere in the label stack except at the bottom. When a received packet contains this label value at the top of the label stack, it is delivered to a local software module for processing.
- A value of 2 represents the "IPv6 Explicit NULL Label." This label value is only legal when it is the sole label stack entry. It indicates that the label stack must be popped, and the forwarding of the packet must then be based on the IPv6 header.
- A value of 3 represents the "Implicit NULL Label." This is a label that an LSR may assign and distribute, but which never actually appears in the encapsulation. When an LSR would otherwise replace the label at the top of the stack with a new label, but the new label is "Implicit NULL," the LSR will pop the stack instead of doing the replacement. Although this value may never appear in the encapsulation, it needs to be specified in the Label Distribution Protocol, so a value is reserved.
- Values 4 through 15 are reserved.

---

[2][ROSE99a] Rosen, Eric C., "MPLS Label Stack Encoding," *draft-ietf-mpls-label-encaps-07.txt*, September 1999.

SUPPORTING TABLES AND MAPS

Several maps and tables are used to support the correlation of incoming labels to outgoing labels and the management label stacks.

The Next Hop Label Forwarding Entry

The Next Hop Label Forwarding Entry (NHLFE) is used when forwarding a labeled packet. It contains the following information:

- The packet's next hop
- The operation to perform on the packet's label stack; this is one of the following operations:
  a) Replace the label at the top of the label stack with a specified new label.
  b) Pop the label stack.
  c) Replace the label at the top of the label stack with a specified new label, and then push one or more specified new labels onto the label stack.

It may also contain information on the data link encapsulation method, and the way to encode the label stack. Both of these topics are explained later in this book.

Incoming Label Map

The Incoming Label Map (ILM) maps each incoming label to a set of NHLFEs. It is used when forwarding packets arrive as labeled packets. If the ILM maps a particular label to a set of NHLFEs that contains more than one element, exactly one element of the set must be chosen before the packet is forwarded. The label at the top of the stack is used as an index into the ILM. Having the ILM map a label to a set containing more than one NHLFE may be useful if, for example, it is desired to load balance the traffic across multiple links.

FEC-to-NHLFE Map

The FEC-to-NHLFE (FTN) maps each FEC to a set of NHLFEs. It is used when forwarding packets that arrive unlabeled, but that are to be labeled before being forwarded. If the FTN maps a particular label to a set of NHLFEs that contains more than one element, exactly one element of the set must be chosen before the packet is forwarded.

AGGREGATION

One way of dividing traffic into FECs is to create a separate FEC for each address prefix that appears in the routing table, as shown in Figure 4–11(a). This approach may result in a set of FECs that follow the same route to the egress node, and label swapping might be used only to get the traffic to this node. In this situation, within the MPLS domain, these separate FECs do no good. In the MPLS view, the union of those FECs is itself an FEC. This situation creates a choice: bind a distinct label to an FEC or bind a label to the union, and apply the associated label to all traffic in the union, shown in Figure 4–11(b).

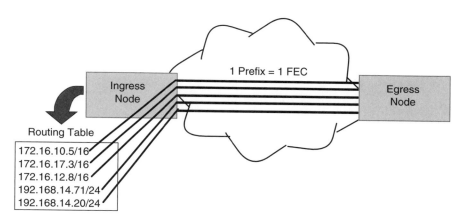

(a) Separate FEC for each address prefix

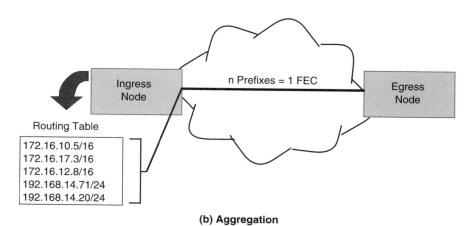

(b) Aggregation

Figure 4–11   Nonaggregation and aggregation.

The procedure of binding a single label to a union of FECs, which is itself an FEC (within the same MPLS domain), and of applying that label to all traffic in the union, is known as *aggregation*. Aggregation can reduce the number of labels needed to handle a particular set of packets, and can also reduce the amount of label distribution control traffic needed.

Given a set of FECs, which can be aggregated into a single FEC, it is possible to (a) aggregate them into a single FEC, (b) aggregate them into a set of FECs, or (c) not aggregate them at all. The MPLS specification speaks of the "granularity" of aggregation, with (a) being the coarsest granularity, and (c) being the finest granularity. The MPLS specification provides a number of rules on aggregation; see section 3.20 of [ROSE00].

LABEL MERGING

With label merging, multiple packets arriving with different labels have a single label applied to them on their outgoing interface (the same interface). The idea is shown in Figure 4–12. LSR C sends three packets to LSR D, with labels 21, 24, and 44 in the label header. LSR D merges these labels into label 14 and sends the three packets to LSR E.

MPLS supports LSRs that have either non-merging or merging operations. The basic rules for these two types of LSRs is quite simple: (a) an upstream LSR that supports label merging need only be sent one label per FEC; (b) an upstream LSR that does not support label merging must be sent a label for each FEC; (c) if an upstream LSR does not support label merging, it must ask for a label for an FEC.

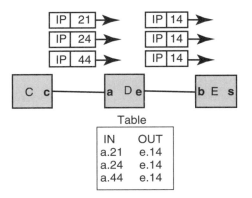

Figure 4–12   Label merging.

Many of the issues surrounding label merging deal with running MPLS on ATM networks. Therefore, we defer the discussion of this aspect of label merging to Chapter 6.

SCOPE AND UNIQUENESS OF LABELS IN A LABEL SPACE

In Chapter 2, the subject of label space was introduced (see Figure 2–5), and Figure 4–13 is another rendition of the Chapter 2 illustration. It shows that labels may be assigned across all interfaces, or to each interface at an LSR.

Given the concepts, Figure 4–14 provides four scenarios of how MPLS sets the rules for the scope and uniqueness of labels. For these examples, MPLS uses the shorthand notation Ru and Rd for LSR upstream and LSR downstream respectively.

- Scenario 1: LSR Rd binds label L_1 to FEC F and distributes the binding to peer LSR Ru1.
- Scenario 2: LSR Rd binds label L_2 to FEC F and distributes the binding to peer LSR Ru2.
- Scenario 3: LSR Rd binds label L to FEC F1 and distributes the binding to peer LSR Lu1.
- Scenario 4: LSR Rd binds label L to FEC F2 and distributes the binding to peer LSR Ru2.

For scenarios 1 and 2, it is a local matter whether L_1 equals L_2. For scenarios 3 and 4, the following rule applies: If Rd can determine, when it

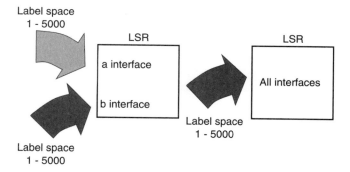

Figure 4–13   Label space.

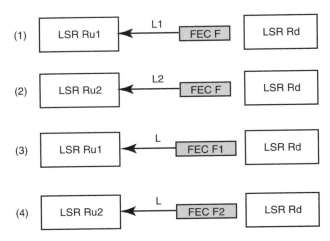

Figure 4–14   Label space and label scope and uniqueness.

receives a packet whose top label is L, whether the label was put there by Ru1 or Ru2, then MPLS does not require that F1 equal F2. Therefore, for scenarios 3 and 4, Rd is using different label spaces for its distributions to Ru1 and Ru2, an example of the per-interface label space.

HOP-BY-HOP AND EXPLICIT ROUTING

MPLS uses two methods for choosing the LSP for an FEC; that is to say, the route selection. One method is hop-by-hop routing, wherein each node independently chooses the next hop for an FEC. This approach is the practice used today in most internets, with a routing protocol such as OSPF. The other method is explicit routing. Each node is not allowed to choose the next hop. Instead, a designated LSR, usually the LSP ingress or egress node, specifies the LSRs that are to be in the LSP.

Two modes are permitted with explicit routing. If the entire LSP is specified, the LSP is "strictly explicitly routed." If part of the LSP is specified, the LSP is said to be "loosely explicitly routed." These modes are similar to IP's strict and loose routing options.

Explicit routing can be a valuable tool to support traffic that has QOS requirements, such as voice and video packets. It is also can play a useful role in traffic engineering operations, a subject covered in Chapter 7.

LABEL RETENTION MODE

At first glance, setting up and using labels appears straightforward. It is indeed just that, if all goes well. But situations may occur that are not amenable to the operations discussed thus far. One such situation is the important consideration of how an LSR makes decisions about retaining or discarding labels. The MPLS specifications set forth these methods for retaining or discarding a label.

- An LSR Ru may receive a label binding for a particular FEC from an LSR Rd, even though this Rd is not Ru's next hop (or is no longer Ru's next hop) for that FEC.
- Ru then has the choice of whether to keep track of such bindings, or whether to discard such bindings.
- If Ru keeps track of these bindings, it may begin using the binding again if Rd eventually becomes its next hop for the FEC in question. If Ru discards such bindings, then if Rd later becomes the next hop, the binding will have to be reacquired.
- If an LSR supports "liberal label retention mode," it maintains the bindings between a label and an FEC that are received from LSRs that are not its next hop for that FEC. If an LSR supports "conservative label retention mode," it discards such bindings.

ADVERTISING AND USING LABELS

A label distribution mechanism is used to advertise and distribute labels, and this subject is covered in Chapter 5. The MPLS architecture specification establishes the overall procedures for these operations, and this part of the chapter provides a description of them. These procedures are defined in Section 5.1 of [ROSE00] and contain many detailed rules. This part of the chapter quotes directly from parts of the working draft to make certain there are no ambiguities in the explanations. In addition, I do not think I can offer a better tutorial on this part of [ROSE00]. I have added illustrations to help your analysis. Figure 4–15(a) illustrates Push-Unconditional, 4–15(b) illustrates PushConditional, 4–15(c) illustrates PulledUnconditional, and 4–15(d) illustrates PulledConditional.

The procedures are executed by the downstream LSR and others by the LSR and are organized as follows:

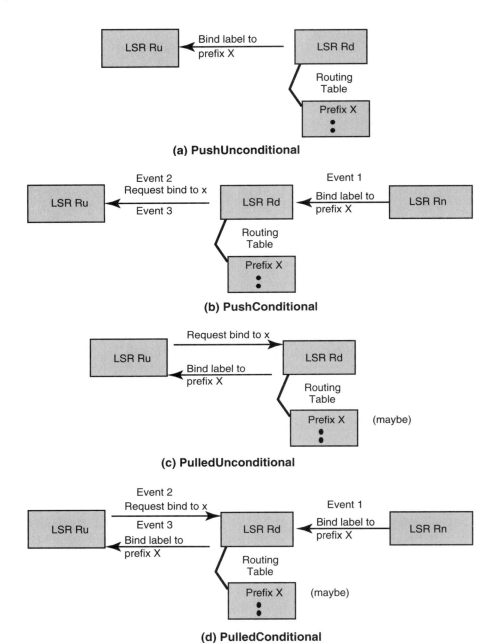

Figure 4–15   Downstream LSR procedures.

Downstream LSR

- Distribution procedure (a) PushUnconditional, (b) PushConditional, (c) PulledUnconditional, (d) PulledConditional
- Withdrawal procedure

Upstream LSR

- Request procedure (a) RequestNever, (b) RequestWhenNeeded, (c) RequestOnRequest
- NotAvailable procedure (a) RequestRetry, (b) RequestNoRetry
- Release procedure (a) ReleaseOnChange, (b) NoReleaseOnChange
- LabelUse procedure (a) UseImmediate, (b) UseIfLoopNotDetected

Downstream LSR

PushUnconditional

Let Rd be an LSR. Suppose that:

1. X is an address prefix in Rd's routing table.
2. Ru is a label distribution peer of Rd with respect to X.

Whenever these conditions hold, Rd must bind a label to X and distribute that binding to Ru. It is the responsibility of Rd to keep track of the bindings which it has distributed to Ru, and to make sure that Ru always has these bindings.

This procedure would be used by LSRs which are performing unsolicited downstream label assignment in the Independent LSP Control Mode.

PushConditional

Let Rd be an LSR. Suppose that:

1. X is an address prefix in Rd's routing table.
2. Ru is a label distribution peer of Rd with respect to X.
3. Rd is either an LSP Egress or an LSP Proxy Egress for X, or Rd's L_3 next hop for X is Rn, where Rn is distinct from Ru, and Rn has bound a label to X and distributed that binding to Rd.

Then as soon as these conditions all hold, Rd should bind a label to X and distribute that binding to Ru.

Whereas PushUnconditional causes the distribution of label bindings for all address prefixes in the routing table, PushConditional causes the distribution of label bindings only for those address prefixes for which one has received label bindings from one's LSP next hop, or for which one does not have an MPLS-capable L_3 next hop.

This procedure would be used by LSRs which are performing unsolicited downstream label assignment in the Ordered LSP Control Mode.

PulledUnconditional

Let Rd be an LSR. Suppose that:

1. X is an address prefix in Rd's routing table.
2. Ru is a label distribution peer of Rd with respect to X.
3. Ru has explicitly requested that Rd bind a label to X and distribute the binding to Ru.

Then Rd should bind a label to X and distribute that binding to Ru. Note that if X is not in Rd's routing table, or if Rd is not a label distribution peer of Ru with respect to X, then Rd must inform Ru that it cannot provide a binding at this time.

If Rd has already distributed a binding for address prefix X to Ru, and it receives a new request from Ru for a binding for address prefix X, it will bind a second label, and distribute the new binding to Ru. The first label binding remains in effect.

This procedure would be used by LSRs performing downstream-on-demand label distribution using the Independent LSP Control Mode.

PulledConditional

Let Rd be an LSR. Suppose that:

1. X is an address prefix in Rd's routing table.
2. Ru is a label distribution peer of Rd with respect to X.
3. Ru has explicitly requested that Rd bind a label to X and distribute the binding to Ru.
4. Rd is either an LSP Egress or an LSP Proxy Egress for X, or Rd's L_3 next hop for X is Rn, where Rn is distinct from Ru, and Rn has bound a label to X and distributed that binding to Rd.

Then as soon as these conditions all hold, Rd should bind a label to X and distribute that binding to Ru. Note that if X is not in Rd's routing table and a binding for X is not obtainable via Rd's next hop for X, or if Rd is not a label distribution peer of Ru with respect to X, the Rd must inform Ru that it cannot provide a binding at this time.

However, if the only condition that fails to hold is that Rn has not yet provided a label to Rd, then Rd must defer any response to Ru until such time as it has receiving a binding from Rn.

If Rd has distributed a label binding for address prefix X to Ru, and at some later time, any attribute of the label binding changes, then Rd must redistribute the label binding to Ru, with the new attribute. It must do this even though Ru does not issue a new Request.

This procedure would be used by LSRs that are performing downstream-on-demand label allocation in the Ordered LSP Control Mode.

Withdrawal Procedure. This procedure is straightforward. If an LSR decides to break a binding between a label and a prefix, the LDP unbinding message must be distributed to all LSRs to which the initial binding was distributed.

Upstream LSR

The upstream LSR operations are simpler than those found at the downstream LSR. They are summarized here.

RequestNever. An LSR never makes a request for a label binding. For example, in Figures 4–15(a) and (b), the downstream LSR takes the necessary actions to bind the labels to the prefixes. It is not necessary to burden the upstream LSR with these tasks. This procedure is applicable when an LSR uses unsolicited downstream label distribution and liberal label retention modes.

RequestWhenNeeded. When a router finds a new prefix, or when one is updated, the procedure is executed—if a label binding does not already exist. This procedure is executed by an LSR if conservative label retention mode is being used.

RequestOnRequest. This operation issues a request whenever a request is received, in addition to issuing a request when needed. If Ru is not capable of being an LSP ingress, it may issue a request only when it receives a request from upstream. If Rd receives such a request from Ru for an address prefix for which Rd has already distributed Ru a label, then Rd assigns a new label, binds it to X, and distributes that binding.

NotAvailable Procedure

If the Ru and Rd are respectively upstream and downstream label distribution peers for address prefix X, and Rd is Ru's L_3 next hop for X, and Ru requests a binding for X from Rd, but Rd replies that it cannot provide a binding at this time because it has no next hop for X, then the NotAvailable procedure determines how Ru responds. There are two possible procedures governing Ru's behavior, RequestRetry and RequestNoTry.

RequestRetry.   Ru should issue the request again at a later time. This procedure would be used when downstream-on-demand label distribution is used.

RequestNoRetry.   Ru should never reissue the request, instead assuming that Rd will provide the binding automatically when it is available. This is useful if Rd uses the PushUnconditional procedure or the procedure; that is, if unsolicited downstream label distribution is used.

Release Procedure

Label release procedures simply mean the binding of a label to an FEC is deleted at an LSR. The scenario for the release is as follows. Rd is an LSR that has bound a label to address prefix X; it has already distributed that binding to LSR Ru. If Rd is not Ru's L_3 next hop for address prefix X, or has ceased to be Ru's L_3 next hop for address prefix X, then Ru will not be using the label, and it makes no sense to retain it unless there is a likelihood of this association reoccurring. Two possible procedures govern Ru's behavior, ReleaseOnChange and NoReleaseOnChange.

ReleaseOnChange.   Ru releases the binding and informs Rd that it has done so. This procedure is used to implement conservative label retention mode.

NoReleaseOnChange.   Ru maintains the binding, so that it can use it again immediately if Rd later becomes Ru's L_3 next hop for X. This procedure is used to implement liberal label retention mode.

Label Use Procedure

Let us assume that Ru has received a label binding L for address prefix X from LSR Rd, and Ru is upstream of Rd with respect to X, and Rd is Ru's L_3 next hop for X. Ru will make use of the binding if Rd is Ru's L_3 next hop for X. If, at the time the binding is received by Ru, Rd is not Ru's L_3 next hop for X, Ru does not make any use of the binding at that time. Ru may however start using the binding at some later time if Rd becomes Ru's L_3 next hop for X. There are two procedures which Ru may use, Use-Immediate and UseIfLoopNotDetected.

UseImmediate.   Ru may put the binding into use immediately. At any time when Ru has a binding for X from Rd, and Rd is Ru's L_3 next hop for X, Rd will also be Ru's LSP next hop for X. This procedure is used when loop detection is not in use.

UseIfLoopNotDetected.   This procedure is the same as UseImmediate, unless Ru has detected a loop in the LSP. If a loop has been detected, Ru will discontinue the use of label L for forwarding packets to Rd. This procedure is used when loop detection is in use, and will continue until the next hop for X changes or until the loop is no longer detected.

SUMMARY

We have examined the major features of the MPLS specification as defined in [ROSE00]. The major features of MPLS have been explained with emphasis on the operations of LSRs and label assignments, swapping, merging, and aggregation. LSP tunnels were investigated, along with label stacks and label hierarchies. We now turn our attention to methods for distributing the labels to the LSRs.

5

Label Distribution Operations

Several methods can be employed to advertise and distribute labels. This chapter examines three methods, the Label Distribution Protocol (LDP), the Resource Reservation Protocol (RSVP), and the Border Gateway Protocol (BGP). The bulk of the material in this chapter is devoted to LDP. This slant does not mean that the other two methods are not viable options. Indeed, RSVP and BGP (with revisions) are quite effective, but LDP is more involved and has more procedures and messages than the other two. This fact is reflected in their descriptions. If you wish to delve into more detail about the subject matter in this chapter, I refer you to Appendix B.

METHODS FOR LABEL DISTRIBUTION

As mentioned earlier in this book, MPLS does not stipulate a specific label distribution protocol.[1] Since several protocols that can support label distribution, are currently in operation, it makes sense to use what is available. Notwithstanding, the IETF has developed a specific protocol to complement MPLS. It is called the Label Distribution Protocol.

---

[1]Some papers call a label distribution protocol a signaling protocol. If this term is used, be aware that it does not refer to conventional signaling protocols, such as ISDN's Q.931 and SS7's ISUP.

Another protocol, the Constraint-Based LDP (CR-LDP), using LDP, allows the network manager to set up explicitly routed label switched paths (LSPs). CR-LDP is an extension to LDP. It operates independently of any Internal Gateway Protocol (IGP). It is used for delay-sensitive traffic and emulates a circuit-switched network.

RSVP can also be used for label distribution. By using the RSVP PATH and RESV messages (with extensions), it supports label binding and distribution operations.

BGP is a good candidate for the label distribution protocol. If it is desirable to bind labels to address prefixes, then BGP might be used. A BGP reflector can be used to distribute the labels.

INTRODUCTION TO LDP

MPLS must provide a standard method for the distribution of routing labels between neighbor LSRs. As of this writing, this standard is being defined in [ANDE00].[2] We will highlight the major aspects of this draft by describing LDP.

We know that MPLS does not make a forwarding decision with each L_3 datagram (based on the addressing and TOS contents of the L_3 header). Instead, a forwarding equivalency is determined for classes of L_3 datagrams and a fixed-length label is negotiated between neighboring LSRs along LSPs from ingress to egress. Routers with label switching capabilities must be able to determine which of their neighbors are capable of MPLS operations. They must then agree upon the label values to be used for the transport of user traffic. The LDP is used to support this requirement.

Figure 5–1 shows the general concepts of LDP. It operates between LSRs that are directly connected via a link (LSR A and LSR B, as well as LSR B and LSR C). It can also operate between nonadjacent LSRs: LSR A and LSR C, shown in the figure with dashed lines. Obviously, the LDP messages for the label bindings for LSRs A and C flow through LSR B, but B does not take action on them.

LSRs that use LDP to exchange label and FEC mapping information are called *LDP peers,* and they exchange this information by forming an LDP session.

---

[2][ANDE00] Anderson, Loa et. al., "LDP Specification," *draft-ietf-mpls-ldp-11.txt,* August 2000.

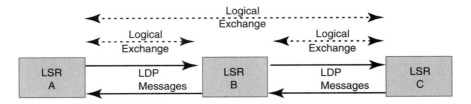

Figure 5–1   LDP message exchanges.

THE LDP MESSAGES

There are four categories of LDP messages, shown in Figure 5–2. *Discovery* messages are used to announce and maintain the presence of an LSR in a network. Periodically, an LSR sends a Hello message through a UDP port with the multicast address of "all routers on this subnet."

The session messages are used to establish, maintain, and delete sessions between LDP peers (the LSRs). These operations entail the sending of Initialization messages over TCP. After this operation is complete, the two LSRs are LDP peers.

Advertisement messages are used to create, change, and delete label mappings for FECs. These messages are also transported over TCP. An LSR can request a label mapping from a neighboring LSR whenever it chooses (say, whenever it needs one). It can also advertise label mappings whenever it wishes an LDP peer to use a label mapping.

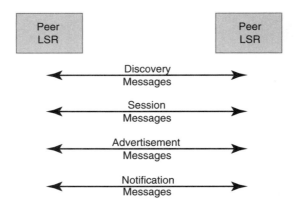

Figure 5–2   Categories of LDP messages.

Notification messages are also sent over TCP and are used to provide status, diagnostic, and error information.

FECS, LABEL SPACES, AND IDENTIFIERS

In Chapter 4, it was explained that user packets are mapped to an LSP, and the method to achieve this mapping is to specify an FEC for each LSP. Earlier chapters also explained that an FEC could be a set of addresses, port numbers, or the PID. LDP takes a more restricted view of the FEC elements and defines two: (a) an IP address prefix, and (b) a host address.

These rules are set forth for the mapping of a specific packet to a specific LSP. Each rule is applied in turn until the packet can be mapped to an LSP.

- If there is exactly one LSP, which has a host address FEC element that is identical to the packet's destination address, then the packet is mapped to that LSP.
- If there are multiple LSPs, each containing a host address FEC element that is identical to the packet's destination address, then the packet is mapped to one of those LSPs. The procedure for selecting one of those LSPs is not defined by LDP.
- If a packet matches exactly one LSP, the packet is mapped to that LSP.
- If a packet matches multiple LSPs, it is mapped to the LSP whose matching prefix is the longest. If there is no one LSP whose matching prefix is longest, the packet is mapped to one from the set of LSPs whose matching prefix is longer than the others. The procedure for selecting one of those LSPs is not defined by LDP.
- If it is known that a packet must traverse a particular egress router, and there is an LSP that has an address prefix FEC element that is an address of that router, then the packet is mapped to that LSP. The procedure for obtaining this knowledge is not defined by LDP.

Label Spaces and Identifiers

Label spaces in LDP are the same as those defined in MPLS, namely the per-interface label space, and the per-platform label space. A label space is identified with a 6-octet LDP identifier. The first 4 bits identify

Figure 5–3   Multiple label spaces.

an LSR and must be a globally unique value, such as an IP address (a router ID). The last two octets identify the label space within the LSR. These octets are set to zero for platform-wide label space.

If the LSR uses multiple label spaces, it associates a different LDP identifier with each label space. Multiple label spaces may be encountered in ATM networks in which two ATM switches have multiple links connecting them, and perhaps reuse the labels on each interface (see Figure 5–3). With this approach, a label space and its LSR is always known if the LDP identifier accompanies an LDP message. In this example, labels 1 through 500 are used twice and the LDP identifiers keep the label spaces uniquely identified.

LDP SESSIONS

LSRs establish sessions between them to advertise and exchange labels. Each label space advertising and exchange requires a separate LDP session. As noted earlier, the LDP session runs over TCP.

Sessions Between Non-Directly Connected LSRs

Chapter 4 introduced the concept of MPLS tunnels and label stacking. Figure 5–4 shows how non-directly connected LSRs advertise labels. We assume LSR A and LSR D wish to set up an LSP between them. LSR B and LSR C are intermediate LSRs between A and D.

LSR A applies two labels on the LSP towards LSR D, labels 33 and 21. In event 1, LSR A learns about label 21 from LSR D. In event 2, LSR A pushes 21 into its label stack. In event 3, LSA A learns about label 33 from LSR B. In event 4, it pushes this label into its label stack.

When LSR A sends traffic to LSR D, it conveys labels 33 and 21 in the packet header. Label 33 is used between LSR A and LSR B, and label 21 is used between LSR A and LSR D, shown in event 5. The other labels used between B, C, and D are not shown in this example. Take a look at

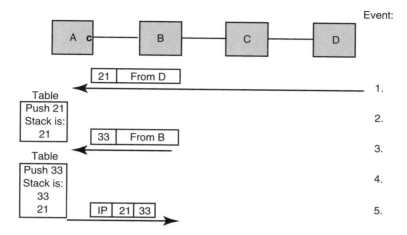

Figure 5–4 Label distribution: Adjacent and nonadjacent LSRs.

Figures 4–8, 4–9, and 4–10 in Chapter 4 if you wish to refresh your understanding of an end-to-end label operation.

How LSRs Know About Other LSRs

LSRs discover each other in one of two ways. The basic discovery mechanism is used when LSR neighbors are connected directly by a link. An LSR periodically sends LDP Hello messages out of its interfaces. These Hellos are sent over UDP, with a multicast address of "all routers on this subnet." The Hello contains the LDP identifier discussed earlier.

The second method is an extended discovery mechanism. The LSR must send a Hello message, called a *targeted Hello,* to LSRs with a specific IP address; the message contains the LDP identifier. These targeted addresses have been discovered by conventional routing protocols.

LABEL DISTRIBUTION AND MANAGEMENT

This part of the chapter explains the LDP conventions for label distribution and management. I summarize Section 2.6 of [ANDE00] here and provide some graphics to amplify the Internet Draft authors' explanations. This material also revisits several of the basic concepts of MPLS introduced in Chapter 4.

An LSR can distribute an FEC label binding in response to an explicit request from another LSR. This is known as *downstream-on-demand* label distribution. It also allows an LSR to distribute label bindings to LSRs that have not explicitly requested them. The MPLS architecture specification, explained in Chapter 4, calls this method of label distribution *unsolicited downstream;* the LDP specifications uses the term *downstream unsolicited.* Figure 5–5 illustrates both downstream-on-demand and downstream unsolicited operations.

Label Distribution Control Mode

The behavior of the initial setup of LSPs is determined by whether the LSR is operating with independent or ordered LSP control, a topic introduced in Chapter 4 (see Figures 4–3 and 4–4). When using independent LSP control, each LSR may advertise label mappings to its neighbors at any time it desires. For example, when operating in independent downstream-on-demand mode, an LSR may answer requests for label mappings immediately, without waiting for a label mapping from the next hop, as shown in Figure 5–6(a).

When operating in independent downstream unsolicited mode, an LSR may advertise a label mapping for an FEC to its neighbors whenever it is prepared to label-switch that FEC. A consequence of using independent mode is that an upstream label can be advertised before a downstream label is received.

When using LSP ordered control, an LSR may initiate the transmission of a label mapping only for an FEC for which it has a label mapping

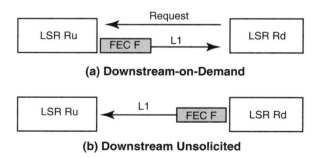

(a) Downstream-on-Demand

(b) Downstream Unsolicited

Figure   5–5   Downstream-on-demand   and   downstream unsolicited.

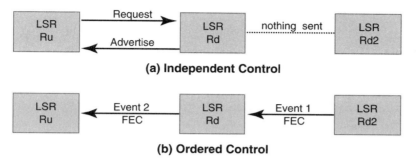

Figure 5–6   Examples of control modes.

for the FEC next hop, or for which the LSR is the egress, as shown in Figure 5–6(b). For each FEC for which the LSR is not the egress and no mapping exists, the LSR *must* wait until a label from a downstream LSR is received before mapping the FEC and passing corresponding labels to upstream LSRs.

LDP MESSAGES

LDP messages are defined in a media-independent format. The intent is that several messages may be combined in a single datagram to minimize the CPU processing overhead associated with input/output. Eleven messages are used by LDP. They are described later in this section. For now, let's examine the conventions for coding the messages.

The LDP Header

Each LDP message (called a *protocol data unit,* or PDU) begins with an LDP header, followed by one or more LDP messages. The header is shown in Figure 5–7. The fields in the PDU header perform the following functions:

- Version: The version number of the protocol, currently version 1.
- PDU length: Total length of PDU in octets, excluding the version and length fields.
- LDP ID: Identifier of the label space of the sending LSR of this message. The first four octets contain an IP address assigned to the LSR, and it is the router ID. The last two octets identify a label

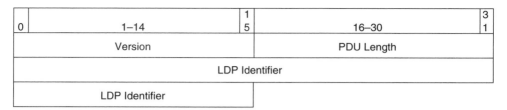

Note: Numbers at the top of the figure are the bit positions of the fields.

Figure 5–7   The LDP header.

space within the LSR. For a platform-wide label space, these fields should both be 0.

Type-Length-Value (TLV) Encoding

LDP uses a type-length-value (TLV) encoding scheme to encode much of the information carried in LDP messages. As shown in Figure 5–8, the LDP TLV is encoded as a 2-octet field that uses 14 bits to specify a type and 2 bits to specify behavior when an LSR doesn't recognize the type, followed by a 2-octet length field, followed by a variable length value field.

Upon receipt of an unknown TLV, if the U bit (unknown) is set to 0, a notification must be returned to the message originator and the entire message must be ignored. If the U bit is set to 1, the unknown TLV is silently ignored and the rest of the message is processed as if the unknown TLV did not exist.

The forward unknown (F) TLV bit applies only when the U bit is set and the LDP message containing the unknown TLV is to be forwarded. If F is clear (=0), the unknown TLV is not forwarded with the containing message; if F is set (=1), the unknown TLV is forwarded with the containing message.

0	1	2–14	1 5	1 6	17–30	3 1
U	F	Type			Length	
Value						

Figure 5–8   The type-length-value (TLV) encoding.

The LDP Message Format

All LDP messages have the same format, shown in Figure 5–9. The fields in the message perform the following functions:

- U bit: This bit is the unknown message bit. If this bit is set to 1 and it is "unknown" (message cannot be interpreted) to the receiver, it silently discards the message.
- Message type: This field identifies the type of message.
- Message length: Length of message ID, mandatory parameters, and optional parameters
- Message ID: A unique identifier of this message. It can be used to associate notification messages with another message.
- Mandatory parameters: Set of mandatory parameters, explained later.
- Optional parameters: Set of optional parameters, explained later.

In principle, everything appearing in an LDP message could be encoded as a TLV, but the LDP specification does not use the TLV scheme at all times. It is not used where it is unnecessary and its use would waste space.

The TLVs: Formats and Functions

This part of the chapter provides a summary of the TLVs. Recall that all TLVs use the format shown in Figure 5–8.

- FEC: This TLV carries the FECs that are exchanged between LSRs. Remember that MPLS and LDP use only addresses for an

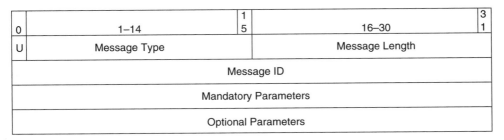

Note: Numbers at the top of the figure are the bit positions of the fields.

Figure 5–9   LDP message format.

FEC, and not port numbers or PIDs. The FEC can be an address prefix, or a full host address. It can also contain addresses pertaining to other networks, such as IPX, but there is little interest in any address other than IP. The FEC may be coded as a wildcard in which case all FECs are identified that previously have been associated with a label. This feature is a handy tool for label withdrawal and label release operations.

- Address list: The address list TLV appears in Address and Address Withdraw messages. Currently, only IPv4 is defined for this TLV.

- Hop count: This TLV appears in messages that set up LSPs. It calculates the number of LSR hops along an LSP as the LSP is being set up. It can be used for loop detection, described in other parts of this book.

- PATH vector: This TLV is also used for loop detection with the hop count TLV in the Label Request and Label Mapping messages. Its use in the Label Request message records the path of LSRs the request has traversed. Its use in the Label Mapping message records the path of LSRs a label advertisement has traversed to set up an LSP.

- Generic label: This TLV contains labels for use on links for which label values are independent of the underlying link technology (a bearer service), such as PPP and Ethernet links.

- ATM label: If ATM is used as a bearer service, this TLV contains ATM VPI/VCI values.

- Frame Relay label: If Frame Relay is used as a bearer service, this TLV contains Frame Relay DLCI values.

- Status: This TLV is used for diagnostic purposes, such as the success or failure of an operation.

- Extended status: This TLV simply extends the status TLV by providing additional bytes for more status information.

- Returned PDU: This TLV can operate with the status TLV. An LSR uses this parameter to return part of an LDP PDU to the LSR that sent it. The value of this TLV is the PDU header and as much PDU data following the header as appropriate for the condition being signaled by the Notification message.

- Returned message: This TLV can also be used with the status TLV. An LSR uses this parameter to return part of an LDP message to the LSR that sent it.

- Common Hello parameters: Recall that neighbor LSRs can periodically send Hello messages to each other to make sure they are up and running. This TLV contains common parameters to manage this operation, such as how often Hellos are sent and received, and how many have been sent and received during a period of time.

- IPv6/IPv4 transport address: If IPv6 addresses are used, this TLV allows an IPv6 address to be used when opening TCP for an LSP session. If it is not present, the source address in the IP header is used. The same idea holds for IPv4 addresses.

- Common session parameters: This TLV contains values proposed by the sending LSR for parameters that must be negotiated for every LDP session. These parameters are

  (a) Keep alive time: indicates the maximum number of seconds that may elapse between the receipt of successive PDUs from the LDP peer on the session TCP connection. The keep alive timer is reset each time a PDU arrives.

  (b) Label advertisement discipline: downstream unsolicited, or downstream on demand.

  (c) Loop detection: indicates if loop detection is enabled or disabled.

  (d) PATH vector limit: indicates the maximum path vector length.

  (e) Maximum PDU length: indicates the maximum length of the LDP PDU.

- ATM session parameters: This TLV specifies the ATM meager capabilities of an ATM-LSR. The options are

  (a) merge not supported

  (b) VP merge supported

  (c) VC merge supported

  (d) VP and VC merge supported

  This TLV provides information about VC directionality, which means the use of a VCI in one direction or in both directions on the link. It also contains a field that specifies the range of ATM labels supported by the sending LSR.

- Frame Relay session parameters: This TLV contains the same type of information as the ATM session parameters, except the TLV pertains to DLCIs.

- Label Request message ID: The value of this parameter is the message ID of the corresponding Label Request message.

- Private: Vendor-private TLVs and messages are used to convey vendor-private information between LSRs.

The LDP Messages: Formats and Functions

This section provides information on the formats and functions of the LDP messages listed below.

- Notification
- Hello
- Initialization
- KeepAlive
- Address
- Address Withdraw
- Label Mapping
- Label Request
- Label Abort Request
- Label Withdraw
- Label Release

Notification Message.   The message is used by an LSR to notify its peer about unusual or error conditions. Examples of conditions are (a) receiving unknown, erroneous, or malformed messages, (b) expiration of a keep alive timer, (c) a shutdown by a node, and (d) failure of an LSP session initialization. In some situations, the LSR may terminate the LDP session (closing the TCP connection). The format for this message is shown in Figure 5–10.

The message ID uniquely identifies each message. It is coded in all messages and is not explained again. The status TLV indicates the status of event, and was explained in the previous section of this book. The optional parameters are these TLVs: (a) extended status, (b) returned PDU, (c) returned message.

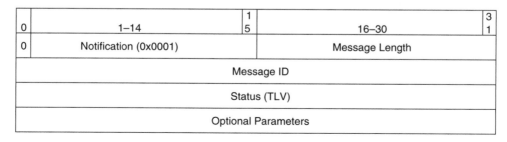

0	1–14	1 5	16–30	3 1
0	Notification (0x0001)		Message Length	
Message ID				
Status (TLV)				
Optional Parameters				

Figure 5–10   The Notification message.

When an LSR receives a Notification message that carries a status code that indicates a fatal error, it terminates the LDP session immediately by closing the session TCP connection and discards all states associated with the session, including all label-FEC bindings learned via the session.

Hello Message. This message is exchanged between two LDP peers during an LDP discovery operation. The format for this message is shown in Figure 5–11.

The Common Hello TLV was explained earlier in this chapter. The format for this TLV is shown in Figure 5–12.

An LSR maintains a record of Hellos received from potential LSR peers. The Hello hold time specifies the time the sending LSR will maintain its record of Hellos from the receiving LSR without receipt of another Hello. A pair of LSRs negotiates the hold times they use for Hellos from each other. Each proposes a hold time. The hold time used is the minimum of the hold times proposed in their Hellos.

The T bit is called Targeted Hello. A value of 1 specifies that this Hello is a Targeted Hello. A value of 0 specifies that this Hello is a Link Hello. The R bit is called the R Request Send Targeted Hellos. A value of 1 requests the receiver to send periodic Targeted Hellos to the source of this Hello. A value of 0 makes no request.

Optional parameters are the IPv4 and IPv6 transport address TLVs, and a configuration sequence number, which is used by the receiving LSR to detect configuration changes at the sending LSR.

Initialization Message. This message is exchanged when LDP peers wish to set up a LDP session. During this procedure, the LSRs negotiate parameters, such as a keep alive timer, the types of advertisement that will be supported (downstream unsolicited or downstream-on-

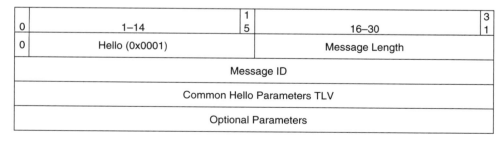

0	1–14	1 5	16–30	3 1
0	Hello (0x0001)		Message Length	
Message ID				
Common Hello Parameters TLV				
Optional Parameters				

Figure 5–11   The Hello message.

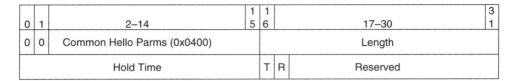

0	1	2–14	1 5	1 6	17–30	3 1
0	0	Common Hello Parms (0x0400)			Length	
		Hold Time		T	R	Reserved

Figure 5–12   Common Hello parameters TLV.

demand). If Frame Relay or ATM labels are to be used during the session, the rules for using these labels are also negotiated. The format for this message is shown in Figure 5–13.

The common session parameters TLV was explained in the previous section. Optional parameters are ATM and Frame Relay session parameters.

KeepAlive Message.   The KeepAlive message is exchanged between peers in order to monitor the integrity of the TCP connection supporting the LDP session. The format for this message is shown in Figure 5–14. There are no optional parameters for this message.

Address Message.   This message is sent by an LSR to its LDP peer to advertise its interface addresses. An LSR that receives an Address message uses the addresses it learns to maintain a database for mapping between peer LDP identifiers and next hop addresses. The format for the message is shown in Figure 5–15.

The address list TLV is the list of interface IP addresses being advertised by the sending LSR. There are no optional parameters for this message.

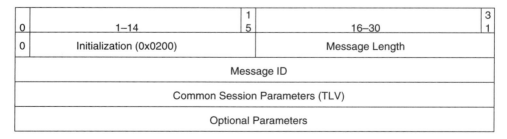

0	1–14	1 5	16–30	3 1
0	Initialization (0x0200)		Message Length	
Message ID				
Common Session Parameters (TLV)				
Optional Parameters				

Figure 5–13   The Initialization message.

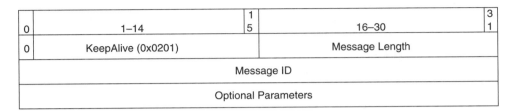

0	1–14	1 5	16–30	3 1
0	KeepAlive (0x0201)		Message Length	
Message ID				
Optional Parameters				

Figure 5–14   The KeepAlive message.

Address Withdraw Message.   This message "undoes" the Address message and withdraws a previously advertised interface address or addresses. The format for this message is shown in Figure 5–16.

The address list TLV contains the list of addresses that are being withdrawn by the sending LSR of this message.

Label Mapping Message.   This message is used to advertise to an LDP peer the FEC-label bindings to the peer. If an LSR distributes a mapping for an FEC to multiple LDP peers, it is a local matter whether it maps a single label to the FEC and distributes that mapping to all its peers or uses a different mapping for each of its peers.

Also, an LSR receiving a Label Mapping message from a downstream LSR for a prefix or host address FEC element should not use the label for forwarding unless its routing table contains an entry that exactly matches the FEC value. The format for the Label Mapping message is shown in Figure 5–17.

Of course, this message must contain the IP addresses and their associated labels. The FEC TLV specifies the FEC part of the FEC-label mapping being advertised. The Label TLV specifies the label part of the FEC-label mapping. The optional TLVs are the Label Request message ID, the hop count, and the path vector.

0	1–14	1 5	16–30	3 1
0	Address (0x0300)		Message Length	
Message ID				
Address List TLV				
Optional Parameters				

Figure 5–15   The Address message.

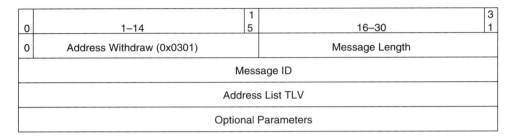

Figure 5–16   The Address Withdraw message.

Label Request Message.   This message is used by an LSR to request that a LDP peer furnish a label binding for an FEC. An LSR may transmit a Request message under any of the following conditions:

- The LSR recognizes a new FEC via the forwarding table, and the next hop is an LDP peer, and the LSR does not have a mapping from the next hop for the given FEC.
- The next hop to the FEC changes, and the LSR does not have a mapping from that next hop for the given FEC.
- The LSR receives a Label Request for an FEC from an upstream LDP peer, the FEC next hop is an LDP peer, and the LSR does not have a mapping from the next hop.

The format for the Label Request message is shown in Figure 5–18.

The FEC TLV identifies the label value being requested. The optional TLVs are hop count and path vector.

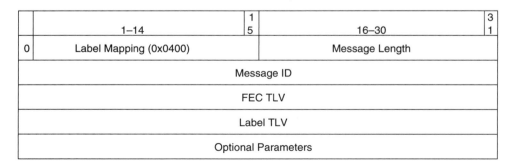

Figure 5–17   The Label Mapping message.

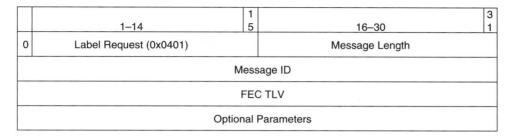

Figure 5–18   The Label Request message.

Label Withdraw Message.   This message destroys a mapping between FECs and labels. It is sent to an LDP peer to inform that node that it is not to continue to use specific FEC-label bindings that the LSR had previously advertised. An LSR transmits a Label Withdraw message under the following conditions:

- The LSR no longer recognizes a previously known FEC for which it has advertised a label.
- The LSR has decided unilaterally (e.g., via configuration) to no longer label switch an FEC (or FECs) with the label mapping being withdrawn.

The FEC TLV specifies the FEC for which labels are to be withdrawn. If no label TLV follows the FEC, all labels associated with the FEC are to be withdrawn; otherwise, only the label specified in the optional label TLV is to be withdrawn. An LSR that receives a Label Withdraw message must respond with a Label Release message. The format for the Label Withdraw message is shown in Figure 5–19. The fields in the message have been explained in previous text.

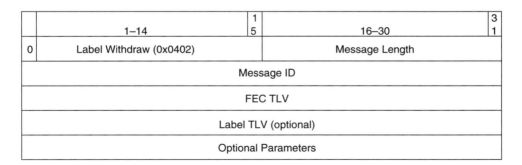

Figure 5–19   The Label Withdraw message.

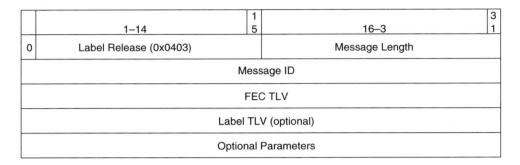

Figure 5–20   The Label Release message.

Label Release Message. This message, depicted in Figure 5–20, informs the receiving LDP peer that the LSR no longer needs specific FEC-label bindings. An LSR must transmit a Label Release message under any of the following conditions:

- The LSR that sent the label mapping is no longer the next hop for the mapped FEC, and the LSR is configured for conservative operation.
- The LSR receives a label mapping from an LSR which is not the next hop for the FEC, and the LSR is configured for conservative operation.
- The LSR receives a Label Withdraw message.

The TLVs of this message have been described in previous text. The optional parameter is the label TLV.

Label Abort Request Message. This message aborts an outstanding Label Request message. There are a variety of reasons for issuing an abort message, such as an OSPF or BGP prefix advertisement that changes the label request operation. The format for this message is shown in Figure 5–21. The contents of the message are explained in previous text, and there are no optional parameters.

RSVP AND LABEL DISTRIBUTION

As its name implies, the Resource Reservation Protocol is used to reserve resources for a session (flow) in an Internet. This aspect of the In-

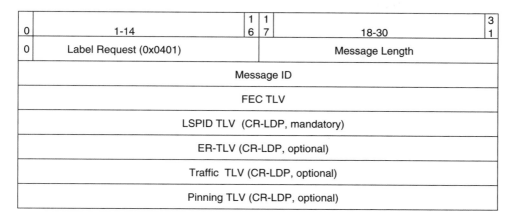

0	1-14	1 6	1 7	18-30	3 1
0	Label Request (0x0401)			Message Length	
Message ID					
FEC TLV					
LSPID TLV (CR-LDP, mandatory)					
ER-TLV (CR-LDP, optional)					
Traffic TLV (CR-LDP, optional)					
Pinning TLV (CR-LDP, optional)					

Figure 5–21   The Label Abort Request message.

ternet is quite different from the underlying design intent of the system, which as we learned earlier, was established to support only a best-effort service, without regard to predefined requirements for the user application.

RSVP is intended to provide guaranteed performance by reserving the necessary resources at each machine that participates in supporting the flow of traffic (such as a video or audio conference). Remember that IP is a connectionless protocol that does not set up paths for the traffic flow, whereas RSVP is designed to establish these paths as well as to guarantee the bandwidth on the paths.

RSVP does not provide routing operations, but utilizes IPv4 or IPv6 as the transport mechanism in the same fashion as the Internet Control Message Protocol (ICMP) and the Internet Group Message Protocol (IGMP).

RSVP requires the receivers of the traffic to request QOS for the flow. The receiver host application must determine the QOS profile, which is then passed to RSVP. After the analysis of the request, RSVP is used to send request messages to all the nodes that participate in the data flow.

RSVP operates with unicast or multicast procedures, and inter-works with current multicast protocols. RSVP requires the receivers of the traffic to request QOS for the flow. The receiver host application must determine the QOS profile, which is then passed to RSVP. After the analysis of the request, RSVP is used to send request messages to all the nodes that participate in the data flow. The path message is used by a server (the flow sender) to set up a path for the session.

Figure 5–22 also shows that the reservation messages are sent by the receivers of the flow, and they allow sender and intermediate machines (such as routers) to learn the receiver's requirements. The PATH message gets things started, and is sent to potential participant(s) of a session. The Reservation (RESV) is sent in response to the PATH message.

PATH and RESV messages contain sufficient information to identify a flow and the QOS requirements for the flow. These requirements indicate a guaranteed service, such as a peak rate for the traffic flow, a burst size, and a token bucket rate, parameters that are explained in the traffic engineering chapter (Chapter 7). Alternately, instead of a guaranteed

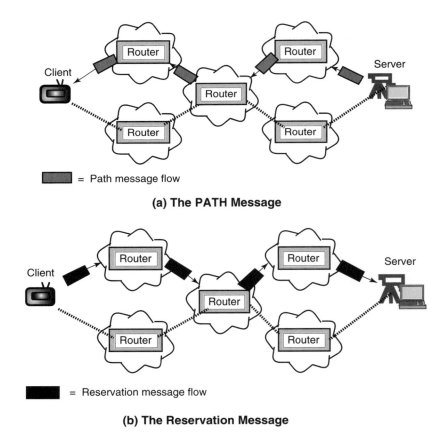

Figure 5–22   The RSVP message flow.

service, a controlled load operation can be executed. With this approach, the network attempts to regulate traffic flow such that one flow does not degrade the QOS of another flow.

RSVP can be used to set up a path and reserve MPLS labels at the nodes between the communicating parties. The extensions to RSVP for this service are special RSVP *objects,* which are fields in the RSVP message.

Figure 5–23 shows the use of the RSVP PATH message and the explicit route object (ERO) that dictates the route through the domain. The ERO is created based on a user's request for the route, or from information obtained from a routing protocol, such as BGP or OSPF. The RSVP session object is used to identify the label switching protocol information, and the RSVP session attributes define a priority for the session.

The RESV message is returned across the same path that its related PATH message took. See Figure 5–24. The function of this message flow is to complete the MPLS route between the users. The labels are assigned, and the label tables are created at each LSR.

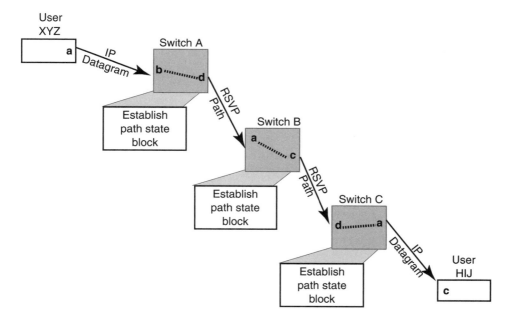

Figure 5–23   Using PATH message for label binding.

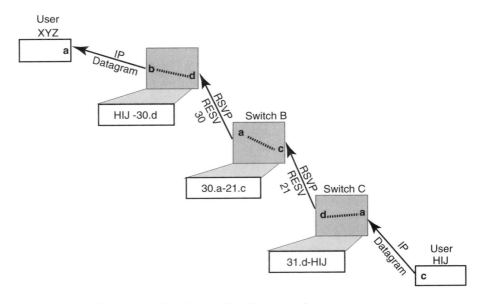

Figure 5–24   Using the Reservation message.

RULES ON USE OF RSVP LABEL OBJECT

[AWDU00][3] provides the rules on the use of the LABEL object, a new object defined for MPLS and RSVP operations. A router uses the top label carried in the LABEL object as the outgoing label associated with the sender. The router allocates a new label and binds it to the incoming interface of this session/sender. This is the same interface that the router uses to forward RESV messages to the previous hops.

In MPLS, a node may support multiple label spaces, perhaps associating unique space with each incoming interface. For the purposes of the following discussion, the term *same label* means the identical label value drawn from the identical label space. Further, the following applies only to unicast sessions.

If a node receives an RESV message that has assigned the same label value to multiple senders, then that node may also assign the same value to those same senders or to any subset of those senders. Note that if a node intends to police individual senders to a session, it must assign unique labels to those senders. Labels received in RESV messages on dif-

---

[3][AWDU00] Awduche, Daniel, O. et. al., "RSVP-TE: Extensions to RSVP for LSP Tunnels," *draft-ietf-mpls-rsvp-lsp-tunnel-05.txt,* February 2000.

ferent interfaces are always considered to be different, even if the label value is the same.

To construct a new LABEL object, the router replaces the top label (from the received RESV message) with the locally allocated new label. The router then sends the new LABEL object as part of the RESV message to the previous hop. The LABEL object should be kept in the Reservation State Block. It is then used in the next RESV refresh event for formatting the RESV message. A router is expected to send an RESV message before its refresh timers expire if the contents of the LABEL object change.

BGP AND LABEL DISTRIBUTION

The Border Gateway Protocol has also been enhanced to support label distribution [REKH00].[4] This part of the chapter provides a summary of the main points of this working draft. If you need background information on BGP, take a look at one of my companion books in this series, *IP Routing Protocols*.

When BGP is used to distribute a particular route, it can also be used to distribute an MPLS label that is mapped to that route. The label mapping information for a particular route is piggybacked in the same BGP Update message that is used to distribute the route itself.

The BGP operations are quite similar to the conventional MPLS label stacking operations. For example, if exterior router A needs to send a packet to destination D, and A's BGP next hop for D is exterior router B, and B has mapped label L to D, then A first pushes L onto the packet's label stack. A then consults its IGP to find the next hop to B—call it C. If C has distributed to A an MPLS label for the route to B, A can push this label on the packet's label stack and then send the packet to C.

If a set of BGP speakers are exchanging routes via a route reflector, then by piggybacking the label distribution on the route distribution, the route reflector can be used to distribute the labels as well. This improves scalability significantly.

Label distribution can be piggybacked in the BGP Update message by using the BGP-4 Multiprotocol Extensions attribute (see [RFC 2283]). The label is encoded into the NLRI field of the attribute, and the SAFI

---

[4][REKH00] Rekhter, Yakov and Rosen, Eric C., "Carrying Label Information in BGP-4." *draft-ietf-mpls-bgp4–04.txt,* January 2000.

(Subsequent Address Family Identifier) field is used to indicate that the NLRI contains a label. A BGP speaker may not use BGP to send labels to a particular BGP peer unless that peer indicates, through BGP capability negotiation, that it can process update messages with the specified SAFI field.

SUMMARY

This chapter examined three methods for label distribution, the Label Distribution Protocol (LDP), the Resource Reservation Protocol (RSVP), and the Border Gateway Protocol (BGP). The bulk of the material was devoted to LDP, due to its many messages and rules.

6

MPLS and ATM and Frame Relay Networks

Since ATM is widely used in wide area networks and performs the job of forwarding traffic (cell switching) through a network, an important aspect of MPLS is its ability to operate over ATM networks, a concept called *overlay*. It is a good idea to be able to integrate IP and ATM operations in one switch, instead of running IP on a router and ATM in a backbone cell switch. This integration is not an insurmountable problem, but it is not a trivial task. This chapter explains how these operations occur, and how ATM and MPLS can interwork with each other. Examples are also provided on using MPLS with Frame Relay.

Several Internet Drafts and RFCs have been published to provide guidance on the interworking of MPLS with ATM and Frame Relay networks. This chapter provides a summary and tutorial on these specifications. The exlanations of Frame Relay follow those on ATM, and are more terse, since many of the Frame Relay operations are almost identical to ATM. In addition, Appendix B provides yet more details on the relationships of MPLS to ATM and Frame Relay.

For more details on this subject, I refer you to these references if you wish to delve into more detail about the subject: [ROSE00], [NAGA00],[1] [WIDJ99],[2] and [DAVI99].[3]

ASPECTS OF ATM OF INTEREST TO MPLS

This section provides an overview of those aspects of ATM that are relevant to MPLS. These topics are of interest:

- Virtual circuits, the logical connections in the network
- VPIs and VCIs, the ATM labels (virtual circuit IDs)
- The ATM cell header containing the labels
- Permanent virtual circuits (PVCs) and switched virtual calls (SVCs)

Virtual Circuits

One task of ATM is to set up a virtual circuit across the network (or networks) between the user machines. In so doing, ATM logically concatenates the physical circuits between the users into the virtual circuit. Each physical circuit that is part of the virtual circuit is called a *virtual circuit segment*. This idea is shown in Figure 6–1.

VPIs and VCIs

An ATM connection is identified through two labels, called the virtual path identifier (VPI) and virtual channel identifier (VCI). In each direction, at a given interface, different virtual paths are multiplexed by ATM onto a physical circuit. The VPIs and VCIs identify these multiplexed connections.

Virtual channel connections have end-to-end significance between two end users, usually between two ATM adaptation layer (AAL) entities. The values of these connection identifiers can change as the traffic is relayed through the ATM network. For example, the specific VCI value has no end-to-end significance. It is the responsibility of the ATM net-

---

[1][NAGA00], Nagami, Ken-ichi et. al., "VCID Notification over ATM for LDP," *draft-ietf-mpla-vcid-atm-o4.txt,* July 1999.

[2][WIDJ99], Widjaja, I., and Elwalid A., "Performance Issues in VC-Merge Capable ATM LSRs," RFC 2682, September 1999.

[3][DAVI99], Davie, Bruce et. al., "MPLS Using LDP and ATMVC Switching," *draft-ietf-mple-amt-02.txt.* April 1999

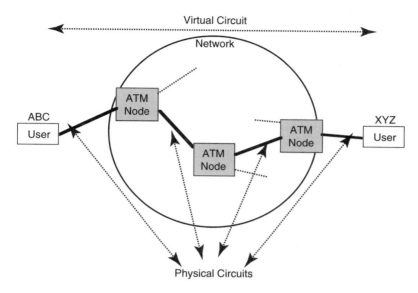

Figure 6–1   ATM virtual circuits.

work to keep track of the different VCI values as they relate to each other on an end-to-end basis. A good way to view the relationship of VCIs and VPIs is to think that VCIs are part of VPIs; they exist within the VPIs.

Routing in the ATM network is performed by the ATM switch examining both the VCI and VPI fields in the cell, or only the VPI field. This choice depends on how the switch is designed and if VCIs are terminated within the network.

The VCI/VPI fields can be used with switched or nonswitched ATM operations. They can be used with point-to-point or point-to-multipoint operations. They can be preestablished (PVCs) or set up on demand, based on signaling procedures, such as the B-ISDN network layer protocol (Q.2931).

Additionally, the value assigned to the VCI at the user-network interface (UNI) can be assigned by (a) the network, (b) the user, or (c) through a negotiation process between the network and the user.

To review briefly, the ATM layer has two multiplexing hierarchies: the virtual channel and the virtual path. See Figure 6–2. The VPI is a bundle of virtual channels. Each bundle must have the same endpoints. The purpose of the VPI is to identify a group of virtual channel (VC) connections. This approach allows VCIs to be "nailed-up" end-to-end to pro-

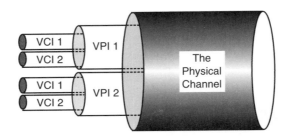

Where:
  VCI = virtual channel identifiers
  VC link = terminated by points where VCI is assigned, translated, or removed
  VPI = virtual path identifiers
  VP link = terminated by points where VPI is assigned, translated, or removed

Figure 6–2   The ATM connection identifiers.

vide semipermanent connections for the support of a large number of user sessions. VPIs and VCIs can also be established on demand.

The VC is used to identify a unidirectional facility for the transfer of the ATM traffic. The VCI is assigned at the time a VC session is activated in the ATM network. Routing might occur in an ATM network at the VC level, or VCs can be mapped through the network without further translation. If VCIs are used in the network, the ATM switch must translate the incoming VCI values into outgoing VCI values on the outgoing VC links. The VC links must be concatenated to form a full virtual channel connection (VCC). The VCCs are used for user-to-user, user-to-network, or network transfer of traffic.

The VPI identifies a group of VC links that share the same virtual path connection (VPC). The VPI value is assigned each time the VP is switched in the ATM network. Like the VC, the VP is unidirectional for the transfer of traffic between two contiguous ATM entities.

Referring to Figure 6–2, two different VCs that belong to different VPs at a particular interface are allowed to have the same VCI value (VCI 1, VCI 2). Consequently, the concatenation of VCI and VPI is necessary to uniquely identify a virtual connection.

The ATM Cell Header

The ATM PDU is called a cell; see Figure 6–3. It is 53 octets in length, with 5 octets devoted to the ATM cell header and 48 octets used by AAL and the user payload. As shown in this figure, the ATM cell is configured slightly differently for the user-network interface (the inter-

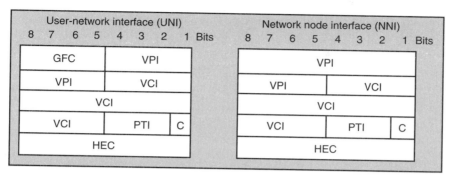

Where:
C: cell loss priority
GFC: generic flow control
HEC: header error control
PTI: payload type identifier
VCI: virtual channel identifier
VPI: virtual path identifier

Figure 6–3   The ATM protocol data units (cells).

face between the user node and the ATM switch) than for the network-node interface (NNI, the interface between ATM switches). Since flow control and operations, administration, and maintenance (OAM) operate at the UNI interface, a flow control field is defined for the traffic traversing this interface, but not at the NNI. The flow control field is called the generic flow control (GFC) field. If the GFC is not used, this 4-bit field is set to zeros.

Most of the values in the 5-octet cell header consist of the virtual circuit labels of VPI and VCI. Most of the VPI and VCI overhead values are available to use as the network administrator chooses. Here are some examples of how they can be used.

Multiple VCs can be associated with one VP. This approach can be used to assign a certain amount of bandwidth to a VP, and then allocate it among the associated VCs. *Bundling* VCs in VPs allows one OAM message to be transmitted that provides information about multiple VCs, by using the VPI value in the header. Some implementations, to avoid processing all the bits in the VP and VC fields, do not use all the bits of VPI/VCI. Some implementations examine only the VPI bits at intermediate nodes in the network.

A payload type identifier (PTI) field identifies the type of traffic residing in the cell. The cell may contain user traffic or management/control traffic. The standards bodies have expanded the use of this field to identify other payload types (OAM, control, etc.). Interestingly, the GFC field does not contain the congestion notification codes, because the name of the field was created before all of its functions were identified. The flow control fields (actually, congestion notification bits) are contained in the PTI field.

The cell loss priority (C) field is a 1-bit value. If C is set to 1, the cell has a better chance of being discarded by the network. Whether or not the cell is discarded depends on network conditions and the policy of the network administrator. The field C set to 0 indicates a higher priority of the cell to the network.

The header error control (HEC) field is an error check field, which can also correct a 1-bit error. It is calculated on the 5-octet ATM header, and not on the 48-octet user payload. ATM employs an adaptive error detection/correction mechanism with the HEC. The transmitter calculates the HEC value on the first four octets of the header.

Permanent Virtual Circuits and Switched Virtual Calls

A virtual circuit can be provisioned on a continuous basis. With this approach, the user has the service of the network at any time. This concept is called a permanent virtual circuit (PVC).

A PVC is established by creating entries in the network nodes that identify the user. These entries contain a unique identifier for the user, which is known by various names such as logical channel, virtual circuit identifier (VCI), and virtual path identifier (VPI). A user need only submit this identifier to the network node. The network node examines a logical channel or virtual circuit table to discern what kind of services the user wants and with whom the user wishes to communicate.

In contrast to a PVC, a switched virtual circuit (SVC) is not preprovisioned. When a user wishes to obtain network services to communicate with another user, it must submit a connection request message to the network. This message usually identifies the originator. It must identify the receiver, and it must also contain the virtual circuit that is to be used during the session. This virtual circuit value is simply a label that is used during this communications process. Once the session is over, this value is made available to any other user that wishes to "pick it out" of a table. Many networks support another virtual circuit service, which is called by various names. I will use the name *semi-PVC*. With this approach, a user is preprovisioned in that the user is identified to the network as well as to the user's end communicating party. Also identified are the network features that are to be used during this session. There-fore, the network node contains information about the communicating parties and the type of services desired.

Figure 6–4 shows how the virtual circuit is initiated by the initial con-nection request message for an SVC. The signaling protocol used to set up the VC is Q.2931. The contents of the message are used at the ATM switches (nodes) to set up a connection and to create routing table entries. Among the fields in the Q.2931 connection request message is a destination address. This address is used by the ATM node to determine the route that is to be established for the connection. Each node accepts the Q.2931 mes-sage, examines the destination address, and then consults a routing table to determine the next node that should receive the message.

The other fields in the message, such as class of traffic, AAL type, and cell performance requirements, are also used to set up the connec-tion and reserve bandwidth for the users.

As each node sets up the calls, it reserves a VPI/VCI for each con-nection. Given an input VPI/VCI value, it selects an unused VPI/VCI value for the output port. The next node receives this value, selects the route, and chooses the VPI/VCI values for its output port, and so on, to the final terminating user device, as shown in Figure 6–5.

It is the job of the network to select values that are not being used on the same physical interface. This approach allows the VPI/VCI values to be reused.

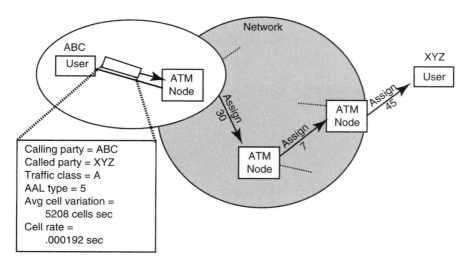

Figure 6–4   Providing the information for the connection.

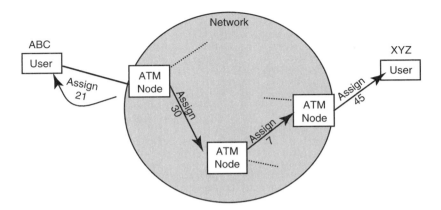

Figure 6–5   Assigning the virtual circuit identifiers.

This figure also shows that the originating users do not give the network a VPI/VCI at the originating UNI. The network assigns these values to the user. This practice varies, but the ATM Forum specification requires that the network take responsibility for assigning VPI/VCIs. The originating end user can be informed of the values it is to use when the network returns a connection confirm message to the user, or with an ATM signaling message.

After the connection is established, the destination address is not needed in the network; only the VPI/VCI values are needed. This idea is shown in Figure 6–6 and should look very familiar, since it is quite similar to the MPLS operations described in earlier chapters. ATM switches use the input port and the incoming VPI/VCI value as the index into a cross-connect table, from which they obtain an output port and an outgoing VPI/VCI value. Therefore, if one or more labels can be encoded directly into the fields that are accessed by these legacy switches, then the legacy switches can, with suitable software upgrades, be used as LSRs. We will refer to such devices as *ATM-LSRs* [ROSE00].

A routing table (also called a switching table, cross-connect table, etc.) is stored at each node and reflects the state of the connection, the available bandwidth at each node, and so on. It is updated periodically as conditions in the network change. Consequently, when the Q.2931 message is received by an ATM node, it knows the "best route" for this connection—at least to the next neighbor node. These operations are dependent on how a vendor chooses to perform route discovery and maintain routing tables.

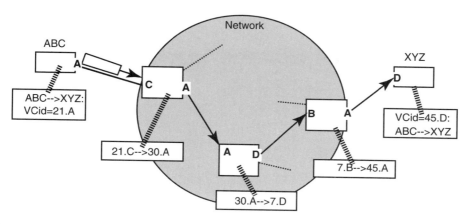

Figure 6–6   Creation of the cross-connect tables.

Where:
   CID = virtual circuit id (VPI/VCI).

SCALING IP/ATM OVERLAY NETWORKS

Recall that the term *overlay* refers to running IP over (actually, through) an ATM network, as shown in Figure 6–7. The important idea is to make ATM invisible to IP and the routers (routers 1 to 6 in this example). The ATM switches set up virtual circuits between themselves and the routers to create a fully meshed router network. The mesh is logical; there need not exist a physical link between each router. The ATM switches in the backbone are tasked with relaying the traffic. This idea is shown in Figure 6–8.

With n routers, the are $n \times (n-1)/2$ potential peer pairs in relation to routing and route advertising, which can translate into substantial over-

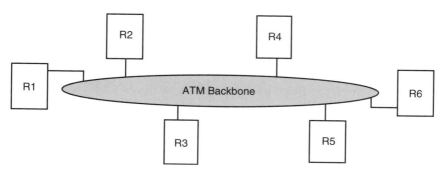

Figure 6–7   IP routers and ATM.

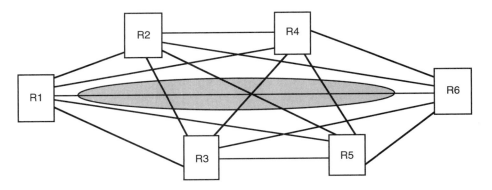

Figure 6–8   Fully meshed routers.

head. In Figure 6–8, six routers are placed on the ATM backbone, with the lines between the routers representing ATM virtual circuits. The potential peer relationships are $6 \times (5 - 1)/2 = 15$. The term *peer* in this discussion refers to the idea of router neighbors and their adjacency to each other. In Internet routing, neighbor routers exchange information with each other about the address of which they are aware. If routing information is sent between the routers across each virtual circuit, then of course for a large network with many routers, the routing updates are going to consume a lot of the bandwidth of the network.

In Figure 6–9, four ATM switches (the boxes in the cloud) are linked to each other and to some of the routers. ATM A switch is directly connected to routers 1 and 2, switch B is connected to routers 4 and 6, switch C is connected to router 3, and switch D is connected to router 5. This approach is much more scalable in that the ATM switches are now running

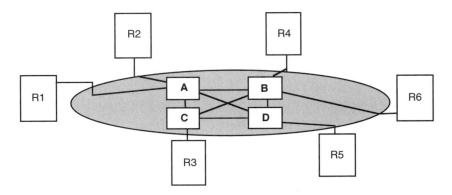

Figure 6–9   Running IP in the ATM switches.

the IP routing protocols (thus IP is overlaid onto the ATM switch). Routing adjacency is now a matter between the ATM switch and its directly attached router.

MAPPING THE MPLS LABELS TO ATM VPIs/VCIs

Figure 6–10 shows three methods for mapping MPLS labels into the ATM VPI/VCI fields. With method A, called SVC encoding, the top label in the stack is encoded into the VPI and VCI fields. Each LSP is correlated to an ATM SVC. ATM's Q.2931 can be used to act as the label distribution protocol. This method is simple, but there is no way to push or pop a label stack since the ATM cell header has only one field (the combined VPI/VCI) to hold a label.

With method B, called SVP encoding, the top label in the stack is mapped to the VPI field, and the second label is mapped into the VCI field. Obviously, two labels are supported, and in addition, the VPI can be used to support VP switching at the ATM-LSRs. For this method, the ATM-LSR at the egress of the VP does a pop operation.

With method C, called SVP multipoint encoding, the top label in the stack is mapped to the VPI field, and the second label is mapped into

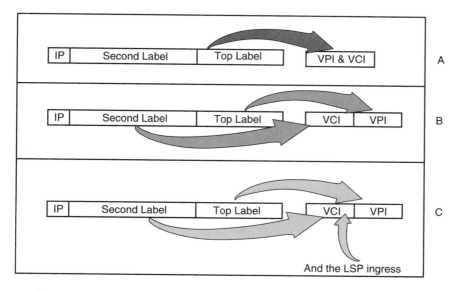

Figure 6–10   Three methods of mapping LPLS labels to ATM VPI/VCIs.

part of the VCI field. The remainder of the VCI field is used to identify the LSP ingress LSR.

With this technique, conventional ATM VP-switching capabilities can be used to provide multipoint-to-point VPs, which allows cells from different packets to carry different VCI values.

TYPES OF MERGING (OR NONMERGING)

Several options are available in dealing with MPLS and ATM labels.

- VP merge
- Non-VC merge
- VC-merge with no cell interleaving

VP merge entails the use of different VCIs within a VP to distinguish different sources. Non-VC merging simply uses a VC to identity each user cell stream.

The third approach is called VC merge with no cell interleave. It requires the LSR to buffer cells coming in from one packet until the complete packet has been received (by an examination of the AAL5 end of the frame indicator). With VC merge with no cell interleaving, the LSR maps incoming VC labels for the same destination to the same outgoing VC label. When VC merge is used, switches are required to buffer cells, so this approach does incur delays at merge points. That is, cells belonging to different packets going to the same destination cannot be interleaved (recall this restriction because of AAL5).

INTEROPERATION OF VC MERGE, VP MERGE, AND NONMERGE

The interoperation of MPLS and ATM with regard to label merging or nonmerging is defined in section 26 of [ROSE00]. First, in the situation where VC merge and nonmerge nodes are interconnected, the forwarding of cells is based in all cases on a VC (using both the VPI and VCI fields). If an upstream neighbor is doing VC merge, then that upstream neighbor requires only a single VPI/VCI for a particular stream. If the upstream neighbor is not doing merge, then the neighbor will require a single VPI/VCI per stream for itself, plus enough VPI/VCIs to pass to its upstream neighbors.

Second, in the situation with the VP merge node, rather than requesting a single VPI/VCI or a number of VPI/VCIs from its downstream neighbor, the LSR may request a single VP (identified by a VPI), but several VCIs within the VP. The packets/cells associated with the VPI all go to the same destination. The use of VCs within the VP permits cell interleaving.

Suppose that a nonmerge node is downstream from two different VP merge nodes. This LSR may need to request one VPI/VCI (for traffic originating from itself) plus two VPs (one for each upstream node), each associated with a specified set of VCIs (as requested from the upstream node).

In order to support all of VP merge, VC merge, and nonmerge, it is necessary to allow upstream nodes to request a combination of zero or more VC identifiers (consisting of a VPI/VCI), plus zero or more VPs (identified by VPIs), each containing a specified number of VCs (identified by a set of VCIs, which are significant within a VP). VP merge nodes would therefore request one VP, with a contained VCI for traffic that it originates (if appropriate) plus a VCI for each VC requested from above (regardless of whether or not the VC is part of a containing VP). VC merge node would request only a single VPI/VCI (since they can merge all upstream traffic into a single VC). Nonmerge nodes would pass on any requests that they get from above, plus request a VPI/VCI for traffic that they originate (if appropriate).

Performance Issues

Non-VC merging is simple and allows the receiving node to easily reassemble cells into packets, since the VC values distinguish the senders. However, each LSR must keep track of each VC label for n sources and destinations for a fully meshed connectivity. This situation presents a scaling problem, since the LSR must manage $o(n^2)$ labels; so, for 1,000 sources/destinations, the VC routing table is 1,000,000 entries.

For VP merging, each LSR now manages $o(n)$ VP labels, clearly an attractive alternative to non-VC merging. But this approach requires more processing on the part of the node to keep track of VPs and their associated VCs.

THE VIRTUAL CIRCUIT ID

The VPIs and VCIs in the ATM cell change as the cell is relayed from node to node. Unlike MPLS and LDP, there is no end-to-end identifier (IP address) in the cell. Therefore, the ATM cell cannot be used to identify a VC end-to-end. In order to use MPLS on ATM links, the ATM VCs must be identified in the LDP mapping messages. For this purpose, the virtual connection ID (VCID) is used. It has the same value at both ends of the VC. [NAGA99] specifies the detailed rules and procedures to communicate the VCID between neighbor ATM-LSRs.

Two categories of VCID notification procedures are defined.

- The inband procedure: the notification messages are forwarded over the VC to which they refer.
- The out-of-band procedure: the notification messages are forwarded over a different VC to which they refer.

NOTIFICATION OPERATION

Figure 6–11 shows an example of an inband notification operation [NAGA00]. The node A establishes a VC to the destination node B (by signaling or management). Next, node A selects a VCID value. Then, node A sends a VCID PROPOSE message, which contains the VCID value and a message ID, through the newly established VC to node B.

Node A establishes an association between the outgoing label (VPI/VCI) for the VC and the VCID value. Node B receives the message from the VC and establishes an association between the VCID in the message and the incoming label (VPI/VCI) for the VC. Until node B receives the LDP REQUEST message, node B discards any packet received over the VC other than the VCID PROPOSE message.

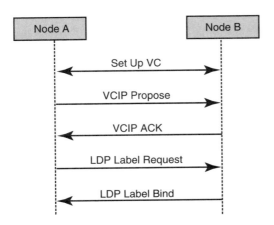

Figure 6–11   Inband notification operation.

Node B sends an ACKnowledgment (ACK) message to node A. This message contains the same VCID and message ID as specified in the received message.

When node A receives the ACK message, it checks whether the VCID and the message ID in the message are the same as the registered ones. If they are the same, node A regards that node B has established the association between the VC and VCID. Otherwise, the message is ignored. If node A does not receive the ACK message with the expected message ID and VCID during a given period, node A resends the VCID PROPOSE message to node B.

Finally, after receiving the ACK message, node A sends an LDP REQUEST message to node B. It contains the message ID used for VCID PROPOSE. When node B receives the LDP REQUEST message, it assumes node A has received the ACK correctly.

The message exchange using VCID PROPOSE, VCID ACK, and LDP REQUEST messages constitutes a three-way handshake. The three-way handshake mechanism is required since the transmission of VCID PROPOSE message is unreliable. Once the three-way handshake is completed, node B ignores all VCID PROPOSE messages received over the VC.

The out-of-band operation is similar, except (typically) an ATM signaling message (Q.2931) is used to carry the VCID. Consequently, the PROPOSE and PROPOSE ACK messages are replaced by the ATM signaling messages.

VPI/VCI VALUES

[DAVI99] establishes the following rules and procedures for the use of VPI/VCI values. When two LSRs are directly connected via an ATM interface, they jointly control the allocation of VPIs/VCIs on this interface. They may agree to use the VPI/VCI field to encode a single label. The default VPI/VCI value for the non-MPLS connection is VPI 0, VCI 32. Other values can be configured, as long as both parties are aware of the configured value.

A VPI/VCI value whose VCI value is in the range 0 to 32 cannot be used as the encoding of a label. With the exception of these reserved values, the VPI/VCI values used in the two directions of the link may be treated as independent spaces. The allowable ranges of VCIs are communicated through LDP.

Connections via an ATM VP

Sometimes it can be useful to treat two LSRs as adjacent (in an LSP) across an ATM interface, even though the connection between them is made through an ATM "cloud" via an ATM virtual path. In this case, the VPI field is not available to MPLS, and the label *must* be encoded entirely within the VCI field. In this case, the default VCI value of the non-MPLS connection between the LSRs is 32. The VPI is set to whatever is required to make use of the Virtual Path.

A VPI/VCI value whose VCI value is in the range 0 to 32 cannot be used as the encoding of a label. With the exception of these reserved values, the VPI/VCI values used in the two directions of the link may be treated as independent spaces. If more than one VPI is used for label switching, the allowable range of VCIs may be different for each VPI, and each range is communicated through LDP.

Connections via an ATM SVC

Sometimes it may be useful to treat two LSRs as adjacent (in an LSP) across an LC-ATM interface, even though the connection between them is made through an ATM "cloud" via a set of ATM switched virtual circuits.

The procedures described in [NAGA99] allow a VCID to be assigned to each such VC, and specify how LDP can be used to bind a VCID to an FEC. The top label of a received packet would then be inferred (via a one-to-one mapping) from the virtual circuit on which the packet arrived. There would not be a default VPI or VCI value for the non-MPLS connection.

ENCAPSULATION AND TTL OPERATIONS

[DAVI99], section 9, defines the rules for encapsulation and TTL operations of edge LSRs. Here is a summary of these rules.

Labeled packets must be transmitted using the null encapsulation of Section 5.1 of RFC 1483. Except in certain circumstances specified below, when a labeled packet is transmitted on an LC-ATM interface, where the VPI/VCI (or VCID) is interpreted as the top label in the label stack, the packet must also contain a shim header.

If the packet has a label stack with n entries, it must carry a shim header with n entries. The actual value of the top label is encoded in the VPI/VCI field. The label value of the top entry in the shim (which is just a "placeholder" entry) *must* be set to 0 upon transmission and must be ignored upon reception. The packet's outgoing TTL, and its class of service (CoS), are carried in the TTL and CoS fields, respectively, of the top stack entry in the shim.

This brief summary is just that, a summary. Other rules are established, and [DAVI99] provides many details on these rules. We now turn our attention to MPLS and Frame Relay. We will see that many of the operations of MPLS and ATM are similar to MPLS and Frame Relay

ASPECTS OF FRAME RELAY OF INTEREST TO MPLS

This section provides an overview of those aspects of Frame Relay that are relevant to MPLS. [CONT98] represents the work from the IETF on Frame Relay and MPLS.[4] These topics are of interest:

- Virtual circuits: the logical connections in the network
- DLCIs: the Frame Relay labels (virtual circuit Ids)
- Frame Relay header: containing the labels
- Permanent virtual circuits (PVCs) and switched virtual calls (SVCs)

Virtual Circuits and DLCIs

Frame Relay virtual circuits are similar to ATM virtual circuits, with one major difference. Frame Relay uses only one value to identify a VC, called the data link connection identifier (DLCI). These ideas are shown in Figure 6–12. Routing in the Frame Relay is quite similar to an ATM network. It is performed by the Frame Relay switch examining the DLCI field in the Frame Relay frame to make a forwarding decision.

The Frame Relay Header

The Frame Relay frame resembles many other protocols that use the High Level Data Link Control (HDLC) frame format. It is illustrated in Figure 6–13. It contains the beginning flag used to delimit and recognize the frame on the communications link. The ending flag signals the beginning of the next frame. Frame Relay does not contain a separate address

---

[4][CONT98] Conta, A. et. al., "Use of Label Switching on Frame Relay Networks," *draft-ietf-mpls-fr-03.txt,* November 1998.

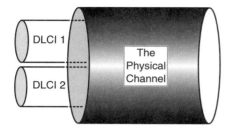

Figure 6–12   Frame Relay virtual circuits and DLCIs.

field; the address field is contained in the control field. Together they are designated as the Frame Relay header. The information field contains user data, such as TCP/IP traffic. The frame check sequence (FCS) field, as in other link layer protocols, is used to determine if the frame has been damaged during transmission over the communications link.

The Frame Relay header consists of six fields. They are listed and briefly described here and explained in more detail in subsequent discussions.

- *DLCI.* The data link connection identifier identifies the virtual circuit user (which is typically a router attached to a Frame Relay network, but can be any machine with a Frame Relay interface).
- *C/R.* The command response bit (not used by Frame Relay).

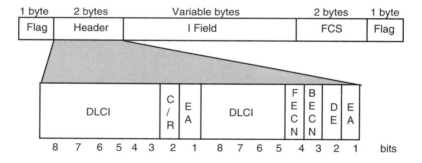

Where:
    BECN: backward explicit congestion notification
    C/R: command/response
    DE: discard eligibility
    DLCI: data link connection identifier
    EA: address extension
    FECN: forward explicit congestion notification
    PDU: protocol data unit

Figure 6–13   The Frame Relay PDU (Frame).

- *EA.* The address extension bits, shown in bit positions 1 in the two octets of the header. Used to extend the length of the DLCI.
- *FECN.* The forward explicit congestion notification bit.
- *BECN.* The backward explicit congestion notification bit.
- *DE.* The discard eligibility indicator bit.

Permanent Virtual Circuits and Switched Virtual Calls

A virtual circuit can be provisioned as permanent virtual circuits (PVCs) or switched virtual calls (SVCs) and are identical to the ATM operations explained earlier. The difference is the DLCI is used to identify the virtual circuit.

Some of the key features of Frame Relay switches that affect their behavior as LSRs are

- The label swapping function is performed with the DLCI. The function is similar to the ATM operation, except Frame Relay has only one value for the label.
- There is no capability to perform a TTL-decrement function as is performed on IP headers in routers.
- Congestion control is performed by each node based on parameters that are passed at circuit creation. The BECN and FECN bits in the frame headers may be set as a consequence of congestion, or exceeding the contractual parameters of the circuit.

SUMMARY

For the foreseeable future, ATM and Frame Relay will be prevalent protocols in wide area networks. This chapter explained the major features of ATM and Frame Relay, and provided summaries of how ATM and Frame Relay bearer services can support a limited set of MPLS operations. The principal problems are the inability of ATM and Frame Relay to support deep label stacks, and their absence of bits to handle TTL operations.

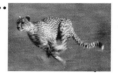

7

Traffic Engineering

T his chapter discusses two aspects of MPLS. The first aspect is how networks in general are engineered to provide efficient services to its customers. The second aspect is how MPLS plays a role in supporting these services.

The chapter explains traffic classes and traffic engineering tools to manage these classes, including policing with token and leaky buckets, traffic shaping with different kinds of queue service algorithms, and induced MPLS graphs. We conclude with examples of how weighted fair queuing (WFQ) is used to manage MPLS flows. If you wish to see how MPLS traffic engineering can be correlated with ATM, Frame Relay, and RSVP, I refer you to Appendix B.

TRAFFIC ENGINEERING DEFINED

Traffic engineering (TE) deals with the performance of a network in supporting the network's customers and their QOS needs. The focus of TE for MPLS networks is (a) the measurement of traffic, and (b) the control of traffic. The latter operation deals with operations to ensure the network has the resources to support the users' QOS requirements.

The Internet Working Group [AWDU99] has published RFC 2702. This informational RFC defines in a general way the requirements for traffic engineering over MPLS.[1] The next part of this chapter provides a summary of [AWDU99], with the author's tutorial comments added to the discussion.

TRAFFIC ORIENTED OR RESOURCE ORIENTED PERFORMANCE

Traffic engineering in an MPLS environment establishes objectives with regard to two performance functions: (a) traffic oriented objectives, and (b) resource oriented objectives.

Traffic oriented performance supports the QOS operations of user traffic. In a single class, best-effort Internet service model, the key traffic oriented performance objectives include minimizing traffic loss, minimizing delay, maximizing of throughput, and enforcement of service level agreements (SLAs).

Resource oriented performance objectives deal with the network resources, such as communications links, routers, and servers—those entities that contribute to the realization of traffic oriented objectives.

Efficient management of these resources is vital to the attainment of resource oriented performance objectives. Available bandwidth is the bottom line; without bandwidth, any number of TE operations is worthless, and the efficient management of the available bandwidth is the essence of TE.

MINIMIZING CONGESTION

Any network that admits traffic and users on a demand basis (such as an internet) must deal with the problem of congestion. The management of all users' traffic to prevent congestion is an important aspect of the QOS picture. Congestion translates into reduced throughput and increased delay. Congestion is the death knell of effective QOS.

Most networks provide transmission rules for their users, including agreements on how much traffic can be sent to the network before the traffic flow is regulated (flow-controlled). Flow control is an essential ingredient to prevent congestion in a network. It is easy to understand the

---

[1][AWDU99] Awduche, W. et. al., "Requirements for Traffic Engineering Over MPLS," RFC 2702, September 1999.

concern network managers have about congestion, because it can result in severe degradation of the network operations, both in throughput and response time.

As the traffic (offered load) in the network reaches a certain point, mild congestion begins to occur, with the resulting drop in throughput. Figure 7–1 depicts the problem. If this proceeded in a linear fashion, it would not be so complex a problem. However, at a time when utilization of the network reaches a certain level, throughput drops precipitously due to serious congestion and the buildup of packets at the servers' queues.

Therefore, networks must (a) provide some mechanism of informing affected nodes inside the network when congestion is occurring, and (b) provide a flow control mechanism on external user devices outside the network.

Two Scenarios of Congestion

Minimizing congestion is one of the most important traffic and resource oriented performance objectives. In this discussion, we address the situation shown in Figure 7–1, wherein the congestion is for a prolonged period, and not one in which there is a short-lived burst of traffic that momentarily exceeds the bandwidth capability of the network.

With this assumption, congestion can be described in two scenarios. The first is straightforward: there are insufficient resources to accommodate the user's traffic. The second is considerably more complex: there are sufficient resources in the network to support the users' QOS needs, but the traffic streams are not mapped properly onto the available net-

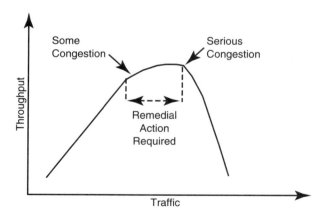

Figure 7–1   Potential congestion problems.

work resources (principally, the communications links between nodes). Therefore, some parts of the network become underutilized and others are saturated with user traffic.

The first problem is solved by building networks with more bandwidth (say, in a freeway analogy, putting in more freeways). We also can help matters by applying congestion control techniques, such as window control operations with "receive not ready," and "congestion notification" (in the freeway analogy, placing traffic lights at the entrance ramps to the freeway). The major problem with the "more bandwidth" philosophy is that it leads to very poor utilization of very expensive network resources during periods when there is less traffic (say, during the early morning hours). It is akin to building a freeway system that accepts all rush hour traffic, and at 2:00 a.m., the 20 lanes of asphalt are almost empty).[2]

The second type of problem, inefficient resource allocation, can usually be addressed through traffic engineering. Alter all, the resources are available in the network. It is a matter of finding them and diverting user traffic to them.

In general, congestion resulting from inefficient resource allocation can be reduced by adopting load balancing policies; that is, diverting traffic to available links and nodes. The idea is to minimize maximum congestion by avoiding that unfortunate curve shown in Figure 7–1. Obviously, the result is increased throughput and decreased lost and delayed traffic.

TAILORING SERVICES BASED ON QOS NEEDS AND CLASSES OF TRAFFIC

Traffic can be organized around a concept called service classes, which are summarized in Table 7–1. These traffic classes are similar to those used in ATM networks. The classes are defined with regards to the following operations:

- Timing between sender and receiver (present or not present)
- Bit rate (variable or constant)
- Connectionless or connection-oriented sessions between sender and receiver

---

[2]An important footnote to this discussion is the view by some people that the building of networks with adequate bandwidth to support any set of users is possible. With the advent of WDM and optical switches, this view is that the concern with bandwidth management will become a moot point. It is a provocative idea, I await the results.

Table 7–1   Classes of Traffic

Class	Features
Class A	Constant bit rate (CBR), TDM-based Connection-oriented Timing required, flow control must be minimal Some loss permitted
Class B	Variable bit rate (VBR), STDM-based (bursty) Connection-oriented Timing required, flow control must be minimal Some loss permitted
Class C	Variable bit rate, STDM-based (bursty) Connection-oriented Timing not required, flow control permitted No loss permitted
Class D	Variable bit rate, STDM-based (bursty) Connectionless Timing not required, flow control permitted No loss permitted

- Sequencing of user payload
- Flow control operations
- Accounting for user traffic
- Segmentation and reassembly (SAR) of user PDUs (protocol data units)

The acronyms TDM and STDM in Table 7–1 refer to time division multiplexing and statistical time division multiplexing respectively. TDM provides a predictable level of service; the user is provided with a constant bit rate flow and periodic slots on the channels, typically every 125 microseconds. STDM provides no periodic slots. The user is given bursts of time on the channel.

TRAFFIC ENGINEERING AND TRAFFIC SHAPING

In its simplest form, traffic engineering attempts to optimize users' QOS needs by making the best use of network resources to support those needs. The limitation, of course, is the network resources. Therefore, with

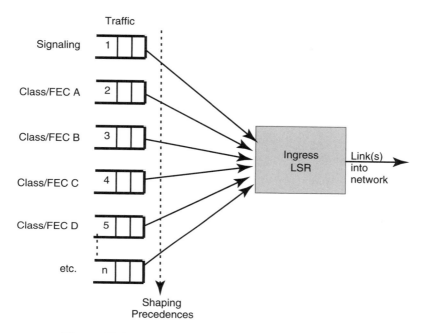

Figure 7–2   Traffic shaping at the ingress LSR.

a network that does not have sufficient bandwidth (link speeds and LSR processing power) to support all users' QOS requirements every moment of the day, traffic engineering operations must "shape" the users' traffic. This means that mechanisms must be in place to determine (shape) how the network supports the different classes of user traffic. As depicted in Figure 7–2, the shaping should occur at the ingress LSR, and entails setting up queues and acting on priorities assigned to the traffic class (giving precedence to one class/FEC over another). In this example, each traffic class is assigned to a different queue, and signaling traffic is given precedence over the other traffic classes, which is a common practice.

QUEUING THE TRAFFIC

Many systems in place today, especially routers, support several types of queues. The prevalent types are

- First-in, first-out queuing (FIFO): Transmission of packets are based on their order of arrival. MPLS uses this method for a given FEC.

- Weighted fair queuing (WFQ): The available bandwidth across queues of traffic is divided, based on weights. Given its weight, each traffic class is treated fairly. This approach is often used when the overall traffic is a mix of multiple traffic classes. Class A traffic is accorded a heavier weight than, say, class D traffic. WFQ is well-suited to manage MPLS flows, and is covered in more detail later in this chapter.
- Custom queuing (CQ): Bandwidth is allotted proportionally for each traffic class. It guarantees some level of service to all traffic classes.
- Priority Queuing (PQ): All packets belonging to a higher priority class are transmitted before any lower priority class. Therefore, some traffic is transmitted at the expense of other traffic.

PROBLEMS WITH EXISTING ROUTING OPERATIONS

In current internets, the routes between sending and receiving parties are set up by routing protocols, such as OSPF and BGP. These protocols are not designed for route and resource optimization, since they a based on shortest path (the fewest number of hops) operations. They build a route based on the topology of the network, not on the bandwidth of the network. In addition, they generally do not consider the class of traffic in establishing these routes. Thus, many networks must adapt schemes to load-balance links and nodes that have not been chosen by the routing protocols.

For example, in Figure 7–3, router A is informed by a routing protocol that it can "reach" host G through two possible paths, one that goes to C first, or one that goes to B first. With a typical routing protocol, the path taken is through C because the path has the fewest number of hops to the destination. That path may indeed be the better one. But if the link between routers A and C becomes congested, or if the link is not a high-capacity link (say, it is an OC-12 link in contrast to the links on the other path that are OC-48 links), then traffic will be concentrated on to the A – B path. The A – C path goes underutilized.

Certainly, we can take measures to "force" traffic to parts of the network that are underutilized. But most networks' communications links vary in their capacity, and it is a huge task to use conventional IP routing techniques to overcome the problem of under- or overutilization of parts of a network. In the complex Internet, IP and the Internet routing protocols have not proved adequate to this task.

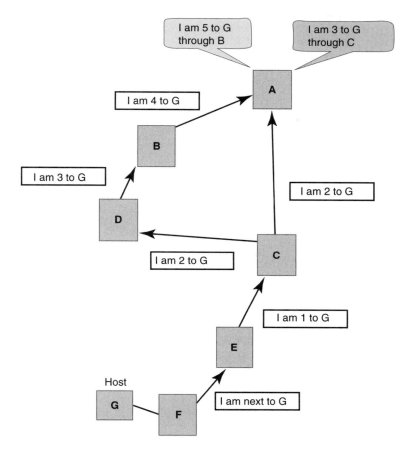

Figure 7–3   The current approach.

THE OVERLAY NETWORK APPROACH

A common approach to ameliorate the problem is to use an overlay network. This approach means running IP over an ATM or a Frame Relay bearer network, and using ATM or Frame Relay virtual circuits as a mechanism to improve network resource utilization. For this discussion, the bearer network is ATM.

The routing protocols are still in operation and are still performing route advertising, but they are not being used (by themselves) to determine the route. By configuring permanent virtual circuits (PVCs) across both paths, the overall operations of the network are improved, as are the services to the network users. In addition, ATM has several features (admission control into the network, policing of traffic, congestion notification, traffic shaping, virtual circuit rerouting, as examples) that provide powerful QOS operations.

Then why not use ATM? The answer is that some engineers think ATM is ill-designed from the standpoint of its consumption of bandwidth (a small payload size of 48 bytes versus a relatively large header of 5 bytes). Others do not like the connection-oriented nature of ATM, wherein a PVC must be set up before any traffic can be sent. Alternately, a connection-on-demand must be made for traffic coming in on the fly, with an ATM switched virtual call (SVC).

These points are well made, but the fact remains that as the Internet evolves, and as the many Internet QOS and label switching RFCs are approved, the Internet will take on many of the characteristics of an ATM network.

One of the goals of an MPLS-based network is to exhibit the power of an ATM network, but not be constrained to the small cells and other vexing attributes, such as ATM's optimal error-checking design for optical fiber links, its inherent use of a label hierarchy (two-level), and its graceful OAM operations with SONET.

Obviously, I am being a bit facetious with my last comments. ATM is an excellent technology, but it is expensive to implement. Alternatives, such as MPLS, look to perform like an ATM network at a lesser cost. It remains to be seen if this will indeed happen.

INDUCED MPLS GRAPH

An induced MPLS graph is analogous to a virtual circuit *logical* topology in the overlay network just discussed. The induced MPLS graph is a set of LSRs (the nodes of the graph) and a set of LSPs which provide the *logical* connectivity between the LSRs. As discussed in Chapter 4, it is possible to use label stacks to create "hierarchical-induced MPLS graphs."

The authors of RFC 2702 establish the rationale for induced MPLS graphs, and their abstract description of these graphs as follows.

> Induced MPLS graphs are important because the basic problem of bandwidth management in an MPLS domain is the issue of how to efficiently map an induced MPLS graph onto the physical network topology. The induced MPLS graph abstraction is formalized below.

Let $G = (V, E, c)$ be a capacitated graph depicting the physical topology of the network. Here, V is the set of nodes in the network and E is the set of links; that is, for v and w in V, the object (v,w) is in E if v and w are directly connected under G. The parameter "c" is a set of capacity and other constraints associated with E and V. We will refer to G as the "base" network topology.

Let $H = (U, F, d)$ be the induced MPLS graph, where U is a subset of V representing the set of LSRs in the network, or more precisely, the set of LSRs that are the endpoints of at least one LSP. Here, F is the set of LSPs, so that for x and y in U, the object (x, y) is in F if there is an LSP with x and y as endpoints. The parameter "d" is the set of demands and restrictions associated with F. Evidently, H is a directed graph. It can be seen that H depends on the transitivity characteristics of G.

TRAFFIC TRUNKS, TRAFFIC FLOWS, AND LABEL SWITCHED PATHS

An important aspect of MPLS TE is the distinction of traffic trunks, traffic flows, and LSPs. A traffic trunk is an aggregation of traffic flows of the same class that are placed inside an LSP. A traffic trunk can have characteristics associated with it (addresses, port numbers). A traffic trunk can be routed, because it is an aspect of the LSP. Therefore, the path through which the traffic trunk flows can be changed.

MPLS TE concerns itself with mapping traffic trunks onto the physical links of a network through label switched paths. Stated another way, an induced MPLS graph (R) is mapped onto the physical network topology (G).

ATTRACTIVENESS OF MPLS FOR TRAFFIC ENGINEERING

Now that some basic concepts have been explained, it can be seen that an MPLS-based network lends itself to TE operations because

- Label switches are not constrained to the conventional IP forwarding dictated by conventional IP-based routing protocols.
- Traffic trunks can be mapped onto label switched paths.
- Attributes can be associated with traffic trunks.
- IP forwarding permits only address aggregation, whereas MPLS permits aggregation or disaggregation.
- Constraint-based routing is relatively easy to implement.
- MPLS can be implemented at less cost than ATM.

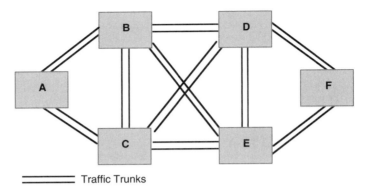

Figure 7–4   Load distribution.

LINK CAPACITY: THE ULTIMATE ARBITER

The MPLS TE model takes into account the fact that the bandwidth capacity of the links in a network are the ultimate arbiter of traffic engineering decisions.[3] To see why this is so, consider that a SONET OC-3 link with a 155.52 Mbit/s capacity can accept an absolute maximum of 353,207 ATM cells per second. Given the assumption that the system is consuming the OC-3 bandwidth perfectly, the following holds: 155,520,000 (less the overhead of the 155.52 Mbit/s OC-3 frame yields a rate of 149.760 Mbit/s)/ 424 bits in a 53-octet cell = 353,207 cells per second.

No more traffic than the 353 kcells per second can be placed on this physical link. Consequently, it is the task of traffic engineering to make efficient use of this link with the following operations: (a) move traffic away from this link interface if the traffic rate is exceeding the link bandwidth rate, or (b) place more traffic onto this link interface if the traffic rate is less than the link bandwidth rate.

LOAD DISTRIBUTION

In many situations, it makes sense to distribute the traffic across parallel traffic trunks, or in some situations, across diverse paths and LSRs in the physical network. For the first operation (see Figure 7–4),

---

[3]This statement is made with the assumption that the nodes (routers) in the network have the capacity to service the links attached to the routers.

multiple traffic trunks are set up between two adjacent nodes (the links between LSRs A – F), allowing each traffic trunk to carry a portion of the total traffic load. This approach is quite common and today is implemented in many networks, such as SS7.

The second operation, distributing the traffic load on diverse trunks and different nodes in the network, is a more complex problem, and it will be addressed later in this chapter.

TRAFFIC TRUNK ATTRIBUTES

MPLS TE establishes the following attributes for traffic trunks.

1. In accordance with the idea of functional equivalence class (FEC), a traffic trunk is an aggregate of traffic flows belonging to the same class, although this attribute is not cast in stone. For example, it may be desirable to place different classes of traffic into an FEC if detailed traffic granularity is not needed.

2. A traffic trunk is capable of encapsulating an FEC between any ingress LSR and an egress LSR.

3. Traffic trunks, through the FEC label, are routable.

4. A traffic trunk can be moved from one path to another, which means it is distinct from the LSP through which it travels.

5. A traffic trunk is unidirectional, but in practice, two of these trunks can be associated with each other, as long as they are created and destroyed together. This association is called a bidirectional traffic trunk (BTT). The two BTTs do not have to traverse the same physical paths, although it may be desirable to do so if the two flows are tightly coupled with regards to real-time interaction. For example, if one traffic trunk traverses through many more LSRs than its partner, it might affect the quality of the interaction. In any event, a BTT is called *topologically symmetric* if the traffic trunks are on the same physical path, and *topologically asymmetric* if they are routed through different physical paths.

Attributes of Traffic Trunks for Traffic Engineering

A traffic trunk has parameters assigned to it that identify its attributes. In turn, these attributes influence its behavioral characteristics, that is, how the traffic is treated by the network. The attribute values are assigned by network administration (provisioned) or by software that automatically examines the FEC criteria (addresses, port numbers, and PID) and sets up the parameters.

The important traffic trunk attributes for traffic engineering are listed here, and described in more detail in this section of the chapter. Some of these attributes are similar to ATM traffic engineering operations, and we will show these similarities as well.

- Traffic parameter attribute
- Policing attribute
- Generic path selection and maintenance attributes
- Priority attribute
- Preemption attribute
- Resilience attribute

Traffic Parameter and Policing Attributes. These two attributes are grouped together due to their close relationships. They are similar to ATM's usage parameter control (UPC). Both MPLS TE and ATM UPC capture the FEC of the traffic, monitor and control traffic, and check on the validity of the traffic entering the network at the ingress node. ATM UPC maintains the integrity of the network and makes sure that only valid VPIs and VCIs are "entering" the network. For MPLS, this equivalent operation would entail monitoring FECs and associated labels.

Several other features are desirable for these attributes:

- The ability to detect noncompliant traffic
- The ability to vary the parameters that are checked
- A rapid response to the users that are violating their contract
- To keep the operations of noncompliant users transparent to compliant users

The Generic Cell/Packet Rate Algorithm (GC/PRA). Many implementations (ATM and the Internet) use the ATM generic cell rate algorithm for implementing policing operations. Figure 7–5 shows the two algorithms available for the GC/PRA, which is implemented as a virtual scheduling algorithm, or a continuous-state leaky bucket algorithm. The two algorithms serve the same purpose: to make certain that cells are conforming (arriving within the bound of an expected arrival time), or

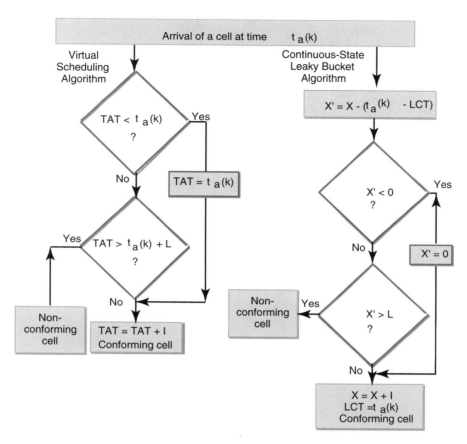

Where:
TAT = theoretical arrival time
Ta(k) = time arrival of a cell
X = value of leaky bucket counter
X' = auxiliary variable
LCT = last compliance time
I = increment
L = limit

Figure 7–5   The generic cell rate algorithm (GCRA).

nonconforming (arriving sooner than an expected arrival time). The algorithm is applicable to cells, frames, packets, and any discrete protocol data unit. For ease of reading, we will use the term *cell* hereafter.

First, two definitions are needed: the theoretical arrival time (TAT) is the nominal arrival time of the cell from the source, assuming the source sends evenly spaced cells. Additionally, the parameter k is the kth cell in a stream of cells on the same virtual connection.

Given these definitions, the virtual scheduling algorithm operates as follows:

- After the arrival of the first cell, $t_a(1)$, the TAT is set to the current time; thereafter,
- If the arrival time of the kth cell is after the current value of TAT—in the flow chart: TAT < $t_a(k)$—then the cell is conforming and TAT is updated to $t_a(k)$, plus the increment I.
- If the kth cell's arrival time is greater than or equal to TAT – L, but less than TAT—in the flow chart: TAT > $t_a(k)$ + L—then the cell is once again conforming and TAT is incremented to I.
- The cell is nonconforming if the arrival time of the kth cell is less than TAT – L—if TAT is greater than $t_a(k)$ + L. In this situation, the TAT is unchanged.

The continuous-state leaky bucket algorithm is viewed as a finite-capacity bucket whose content drains out at a continuous rate of 1 unit of content per time unit. Its content is increased by the increment I for each conforming cell. Simply stated, if at cell arrival, the content of the bucket is less than or equal to the limit L, the cell is conforming. Otherwise, it is nonconforming. The bucket capacity is L + I (the upper bound on the counter).

The continuous-state leaky bucket algorithm operates as follows:

- At the arrival of the first cell $t_a(1)$, the content of the bucket X is set to 0, and the last conformance time (LCT) is set to $t_a(1)$.
- At the arrival of the kth cell, $t_a(k)$, the content of the bucket is updated to the value X′. With this update, X′ equals the content of the bucket X, after the arrival of the last conforming cell minus the amount the bucket has drained since that arrival—in the flow chart: X′ = X – $t_a(k)$ – LCT.
- The content of the bucket is not allowed to be negative—in the flow chart: X′ < 0, then X′ = 0.
- If X′ is less than or equal to the limit value L, then the cell is conforming and the content of the bucket X is set to X′ + I for the current cell and the LCT is set to current time $t_a(k)$.
- If X′ is greater than L, then the cell is nonconforming and the values of X and LCT are not changed.

Generic Path Selection and Management Attribute. This attribute is concerned with the selection of the route taken by the traffic trunk and the rules for the maintenance of paths that have been established. The paths can be derived from conventional routing protocols, such as OSPF or BGP, or they can be preconfigured (administratively specified explicit paths). For MPLS networks, a "path preference rule" is associated with an administratively specified path and is set up as mandatory or nonmandatory.

Resource class affinity attributes associated with a traffic trunk can be used to specify the class of resources that are to be explicitly included or excluded from the path of the traffic trunk. These policy attributes can be used to impose additional constraints on the path traversed by a given traffic trunk. Resource class affinity attributes for traffic can be specified as a sequence of tuples:

<resource-class, affinity>; <resource-class, affinity>; ..

The resource class parameter identifies a resource class for which an affinity relationship is defined with respect to the traffic trunk. The affinity parameter indicates the affinity relationship; that is, whether members of the resource class are to be included or excluded from the path of the traffic trunk. The affinity parameter may be a binary variable, which takes one of the following values: (1) explicit inclusion, and (2) explicit exclusion.

An adaptivity attribute is a part of the path maintenance parameters associated with traffic trunks. The adaptivity attribute associated with a traffic trunk indicates whether the trunk is subject to reoptimization. An adaptivity attribute is a binary variable which takes one of the following values: (1) permit reoptimization, and (2) disable reoptimization.

Priority Attribute. This attribute is used to define the relative importance of traffic trunks and is quite important if constraint-based routing is used in the network. This attribute is discussed in more detail later in this chapter and in Chapter 8.

Preemption Attribute. The preemption attribute determines whether a traffic trunk can preempt another traffic trunk from a given path, and whether another trunk can preempt a specific traffic trunk. Preemption is useful for both traffic oriented and resource oriented performance objectives. Preemption assures that high priority traffic trunks can always be routed through relatively favorable paths within a differentiated services environment. Preemption can also be used to implement various prioritized restoration policies following fault events.

These MPLS concepts are very similar to SS7 rules on its signaling link selection rules. With MPLS, the preemption attribute can be used to specify four preempt modes for a traffic trunk: (1) preemptor enabled, (2) non-preemptor, (3) preemptable, and (4) non-preemptable. A preemptor enabled traffic trunk can preempt lower priority traffic trunks designated as preemptable. A traffic specified as non-preemptable cannot be preempted by any other trunks, regardless of relative priorities. A traffic trunk designated as preemptable can be preempted by higher priority trunks that are preemptor enabled.

Some of the preempt modes are mutually exclusive. Using the numbering scheme depicted above, the feasible preempt mode combinations for a given traffic trunk are as follows: (1, 3), (1, 4), (2, 3), and (2, 4). The (2, 4) combination should be the default.

A traffic trunk, say A, can preempt another traffic trunk, say B, only if all of the following five conditions hold:

1. A has a relatively higher priority than B
2. A contends for a resource utilized by B
3. the resource cannot concurrently accommodate A and B based on certain decision criteria
4. A is preemptor enabled
5. B is preemptable

Resilience Attribute.   The resilience attribute determines the behavior of a traffic trunk under fault conditions; that is, when a fault occurs along the path through which the traffic trunk traverses. The basic problems that need to be addressed under such circumstances are (1) fault detection, (2) failure notification, (3) recovery and service restoration.

CONSTRAINT-BASED ROUTING (CR)

Constraint-based routing (also called QOS routing) is designed to provide a route through the MPLS network based on a user's QOS needs. It is demand-driven and is aware of the traffic trunk attributes and the attributes of network resources. Each LSR automatically computes an explicit route for each traffic trunk based on the requirements of the trunk's attributes, subject to the constraints of network resources and the administrative policies of the network.

ATM and Frame Relay networks have been using constraint-based routing for a number of years. Work is underway to extend these concepts for layer 3 operations. The focus is on extending OSPF and IS-IS to support constraint-based routing. For more information on using OSPF, see RFC 2676. Chapter 9 explains constraint-based routing operations using LDP. This part of the chapter explains the parameters that are exchanged between constraint-based LSRs (CR-LSRs) and how they are used by these LSRs, and [JAMO99] has more details if you need them.

Peak Rate

The peak rate defines the maximum rate at which traffic should be sent to the CR-LSP. The peak rate is useful for the purpose of resource allocation. If resource allocation within the MPLS domain depends on the peak rate value, then it should be enforced at the ingress to the MPLS domain.

Committed Rate

The committed rate defines the rate that the MPLS domain commits to be available to the CR-LSP.

Excess Burst Size

The excess burst size (EBS) may be used at the edge of an MPLS domain for the purpose of traffic conditioning. The excess burst size may be used to measure the extent by which the traffic sent on a CR-LSP exceeds the committed rate. The possible traffic conditioning actions, such as passing, marking or dropping, are specific to the MPLS domain, and are explained in Chapter 8.

Peak Rate Token Bucket

We examined the token bucket concept earlier. For MPLS, it is defined as follows. The peak rate of a CR-LSP is specified in terms of a token bucket P with token rate PDR and maximum token bucket size PBS.

The token bucket P is initially (at time 0) full, i.e., the token count $Tp(0) = PBS$. Thereafter, the token count Tp, if less than PBS, is incremented by one PDR times per second. When a packet of size B bytes arrives at time t, the following happens:

- If $Tp(t)-B > = 0$, the packet is not in excess of the peak rate and Tp is decremented by B down to the minimum value of 0, else
- The packet is in excess of the peak rate and Tp is not decremented.

According to the above definition, a positive infinite value of either PDR or PBS implies that arriving packets are never in excess of the peak rate.

Committed Data Rate Token Bucket

The committed rate of a CR-LSP is specified in terms of a token bucket C with a committed data rate (CDR). The extent by which the offered rate exceeds the committed rate may be measured in terms of another token bucket E, which also operates at rate CDR. The maximum size of the token bucket C is a committed burst size (CBS) and the maximum size of the token bucket E is EBS.

The token buckets C and E are initially (at time 0) full, i.e., the token count $Tc(0) = CBS$ and the token count $Te(0) = EBS$. Thereafter, the token counts Tc and Te are updated CDR times per second as follows:

- If Tc is less than CBS, Tc is incremented by one, else
- If Te is less then EBS, Te is incremented by one, else
- Neither Tc nor Te is incremented.

When a packet of size B bytes arrives at time t, the following happens:

- If $Tc(t)-B > = 0$, the packet is not in excess of the committed rate and Tc is decremented by B down to the minimum value of 0, else
- If $Te(t)-B >= 0$, the packet is in excess of the committed rate but is not in excess of the EBS and Te is decremented by B down to the minimum value of 0, else
- The packet is in excess of both the committed rate and the EBS, and neither Tc nor Te is decremented.

Weight

The weight determines the CR-LSP's relative share of the possible excess bandwidth above its committed rate. This definition is different from our earlier definition of weighted fair queuing, and the two should not be confused. Later in this chapter, examples are provided of how weighted fair queuing can be applied to MPLS flows.

DIFFERENTIATED SERVICES, MPLS, AND TRAFFIC ENGINEERING

Chapter 8 discusses the role of MPLS in supporting differentiated services (DS). Since DS is concerned with providing QOS to network users, it must be concerned with network performance. This section explains how DS approaches traffic engineering operations.

Average Rate Meter

This meter measures the rate that packets are submitted to it over a specified time interval, for example 1000 packets per second for a one second interval. If the total number of packets that arrive between the current time T, and T-1 second do not exceed 1000, the packet under consideration is conforming. Otherwise, the packet is non-conforming.

Exponential Weighted Moving Average Meter

The exponential weighted moving average (EWMA) meter is expressed as follows:

$$avg\,(n+1) = (1 - Gain) * avg\,(n) + Gain * actual\,(n + 1)$$
$$t\,(n+1) = t\,(n) + \Delta$$

where n is the number of packets, and actual (n) and avg (n) measure the number of bytes in the incoming packets in a small sampling interval, Δ.

Gain controls the frequency response of a low-pass filter operation. An arriving packet that pushes the average rate over a predefined rate Average Rate is non-conforming.

So, for a packet arriving at time t (m):

```
if (avg (m) > AverageRate)
    nonconforming
else
    conforming
```

Token Bucket Meter

The token bucket meter is similar to the ATM token bucket explained earlier in this chapter. Let's review the token bucket (TB) meter as defined in [BERN99].

- The TB profile contains three parameters: (a) an average rate, (b) a peak rate, and (c) a burst size.
- The meter compares packet arrival rate to average rate as byte tokens accumulate in the bucket at the average rate.
- Byte tokens accumulate in the bucket at the average rate, up to a maximum burst size (a credit).
- Arriving packets of L length are conforming if L tokens are available in the bucket at the time of packet arrival.
- Packets are allowed to the average rate in bursts up to the burst size, as long as they do not exceed the peak rate, at which point the bucket is drained.
- Arriving packets of L length are nonconforming if insufficient L tokens are in the bucket upon the packet arrival.

It is possible to implement token bucket models that have more than one burst size and conformance level; for example, two burst sizes and three conformance level. This concept is known as two-level token bucket meter and is similar to Frame Relay's committed burst (Bc) and excess burst (Be) profiles.

IDEAS ON SHAPING OPERATIONS

We learned that the shapers (at the ingress LSR) condition, or shape, traffic to a certain temporal profile. For example, in an average rate meter operation in which 1,000 packets are submitted over a one-second interval, the 1001st arrival of a packet within the one-second interval would require the packet to be held in buffer until it becomes conforming. Alternately, it might be marked and possibly discarded.

Shaping operations can be complex. They must be able to prevent a "rogue" flow from seizing more QOS resources that it is allowed. Also, they must not allow conformant flows to be compromised by the rogue flows. In many instances, the shaping operations depend on the size of buffers and on queue depths. However, the shaper's individual actions are straightforward, with the use of, say, token buckets, and so on.

DS Guaranteed Rate

The Internet Network Working Group has been working on specifications to define a DS guaranteed rate per-hop behavior (PHB)

[WORS98];[4] see Figure 7–6. The concepts revolve around non-real time traffic with a guaranteed rate (GR). This rate is also defined in ATM as part of the available bit rate (ABR) service. One difference between the ATM and DS approaches is that ATM is constrained to defining a successful delivery as one in which all the bits in the user frame are delivered successfully, which may entail more than one successfully delivered cell. This distinction is avoided in DS because the DS operations are defined at the L_3 IP level. The following is an overview of the DS GR, as defined in [WORS98].

The GR service provides transport of IP data with a minimum bit rate guarantee under the assumption of a given burst limit.

GR implies that if the user sends bursts of packets, which in total do not exceed the maximum burst limit, then the user should expect to see all of these packets delivered with minimal loss. GR also allows the user to send in excess of the committed rate and the associated burst limit, but the excess traffic will only be delivered within the limits of available resources.

For excess traffic, each user should have access to a fair share of available resources. The definition of fair share is network-specific and is not specified by either the GR PHB or service. The DS GR uses the term *service representation* (SR) to describe a guaranteed minimum rate and the packet characteristics to which the DS GR service commitment applies. The guaranteed minimum rate uses the generic packet rate algorithm (GPRA) leaky bucket with the rate and credit parameter GPRA *(x, y),* where *x* is the rate parameter in bytes per second, and *y* is the credit limit parameter in bytes.

The SR is defined by (S, CR, BL), where S is the set of characteristics of the packet stream to which the service is being committed. The guaranteed minimum rate specification is defined as GPRA (CR, BL), where CR is the committed rate in bit/s and BL is the burst limit in bytes.

The interpretation of the SR is: The network commits to transporting with minimal loss at least those packets belonging to the stream specified by S that pass a hypothetical implementation of the GPRA (CR, BL) located at the network's ingress interface.

The following theorem ensures a DS GR level of service that is always at least R as defined in the GR PHB, and I quote directly from Worster [WORS98]:

---

[4][WORS98] Worster, Tom, Wentworth, Robert. "Guaranteed Rate in Differentiated Services," draft-worster-diffserv-gr-00.txt, June 1998.

Let a_j be the arrival time of the start of packet j, let t_j be the time when the start of packet j is transmitted, and let TL_j be the total length of packet j. Suppose the transmission times satisfy s_j < t_j < s_j + T_2, where s_(j+1) − s_j <= (TL_j/R), and also suppose that if a packet arrives when no other packets in the stream are awaiting transmission, then a_j + T_0 <= s_j < a_j + T_0 + T_1. T_0, T_1, and T_2 are, respectively, the fixed empty-queue packet latency, the maximum variation in the empty-queue packet latency, and the scheduling tolerance. Then, if the arriving packets all pass GPRA(R, B), the transmitted packets will all pass GPRA(R, (B + (T_0 + T_1)*R)).

The proof for this theorem is found in an ATM Forum paper by [WENT97].[5]

Though perhaps not all "guaranteed rate" nodes will schedule packets in a way that fits this form, the preceding theorem suggests that it is reasonable to expect that a significant class of such devices would have the ability to guarantee that if the input packet stream satisfies GPRA(R, B), then the output packet stream will satisfy GPRA(R, B + BTI), where BTI is the device's burst tolerance increment for the stream in question. This result allows us to consider several possible schemes by which an edge-to-edge guaranteed rate service commitment may be made. For example, if we know that each node has a BTI that does not exceed BTI_max, then we can establish GR service with parameters {S, CR, and BL} by provisioning a GR PHB with parameters {S, R = CR, and B = BL + BTI_max} along the stream's path through the network. We do not attempt to specify the rules by which a network operator should distribute appropriate GR PHB parameters. To some extent, the appropriate scheme will depend on characteristics of the implementation of the GR PBH in network nodes. It may also depend on limitations of the protocol used to distribute the parameters. GR service can also be supported across concatenated GR diff-serv networks.

Assured and Expedited Forwarding PHBs

The Internet Network Working Group has recognized that additional PHBs must be defined for DiffServ nodes to support a diverse user community. To that end [JACO99][6] has authored the RFC 2598 "An Expedited Forwarding (EF) PHB," and [HEIN99][7] has authored the RFC 2597 "Assured Forwarding PHB Group."

The codepoint (explained in Chapter 8) for the expedited forwarding (EF) is 101110. The DS traffic conditioning block must treat the EF PHB

---

[5][WENT97] Wentworth, R., ATM Forum Contribution 97–0980, December 1997.
[6][JACO99] Jacobson, V. et al., RFC 2598, "An Expedited Forwarding PHB," June 1999.
[7][HEIN99] Heinanen, J. et al., RFC 2597, "Assured Forwarding PHB Group," June 1999.

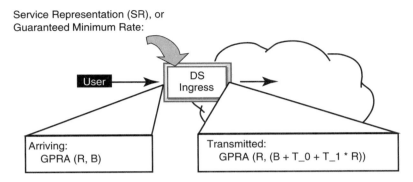

Figure 7–6   **DiffServ guaranteed rate (GR).**

as the highest priority of all traffic. However, EF packets are not allowed
to preempt other traffic. Consequently, a tool, such as a token bucket,
must be part of the DS features. RFC 2598 includes an appendix (Appendix A) that explains the results of some simulations of models to support
EF PHB. I found this information very useful in my work, and I recom-
mend you read it.

EXAMPLES OF WFQ AND MPLS FLOWS

We conclude this chapter by providing some examples of how WFQ
can be used to allocate bandwidth among different MPLS flows. Recall
that WFQ assigns a weight to each flow; it is "precedence" aware and determines the transmit order for queued packets.

We will use the example cited earlier. Let's review it. A SONET
OC 3 link in Figure 7–7 with a 155.52 Mbit/s capacity can accept an absolute maximum of 353,207 ATM cells per second. Given the assumption
that the system is consuming the OC-3 bandwidth perfectly (which depends on the efficiency of the LSR), the following holds: 155,520,000 (less
the overhead of the 155.52 Mbit/s OC-3 frame yields a rate of 149.760
Mbit/s)/ 424 bits in a 53-octet cell = 353,207 cells per second).

Eight levels of priority are permitted. There are eight levels because
(a) the IP TOS precedence field is 3-bits, and could be used by the user

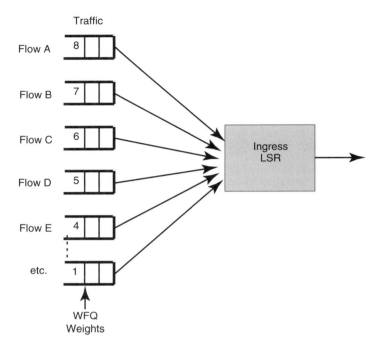

Figure 7–7   WFQ and MPLS.

application to signal to the network the user's precedence needs, and (b) the MPLS shim header Exp field is also 3-bits and can carry the TOS precedence bits. In addition, Cisco routers use this approach for native-mode IP packets.

For this example, all eight queues are to be serviced every second. Based on the weights assigned to the eight queues, n number of cells will be extracted from each queue and sent onto the SONET link. The limit is 353,207 cells during the one-second service cycle.

A single flow is in each queue; each flow receives part of the bandwidth based on this simple scheme:

Total Weights: 8+7+6+5+4+3+2+1 = 36

The MPLS flow in the highest precedence queue is accorded 8/36 of the bandwidth. The MPLS flow in the lowest precedent queue is accorded 1/36 of the bandwidth. Translating these functions to percentages,

8/36 = .222 and 1/36 = .027

Consequently, flow A gets 78,411 cells extracted from its queue during the service cycle, almost one-quarter of the total capacity of the link. The lowest precedence flow has 9,536 cells serviced. Keep in mind that each flow likely consists of more than one end user traffic flow. After all, that is one purpose of MPLS: to aggregate flows.

WFQ is more flexible than the operations shown in this example. Let's assume multiple flows are associated with the eight traffic classes, and it is still desirable to allocate bandwidth fairly among all flows. For this example, the FEC class (and associated flow) is inferred from the MPLS label, and perhaps the Exp field. Therefore, many flows can be identified. As shown in Figure 7–8, four flows are associated with precedence 5, two flows with precedence 4, and one flow with the others.

$$8+7+6+5(4)+4(2)+3+2+1 = 55$$

With this set of flows, each flow in precedence 5 gets 5/55 of the bandwidth (32,109 cells per second for each flow), and each flow in precedence 4 gets 4/55 (25,687 cells per second for each flow). The one flow in queue A (Flow A) gets 8155 (51,215 cells) of the bandwidth.

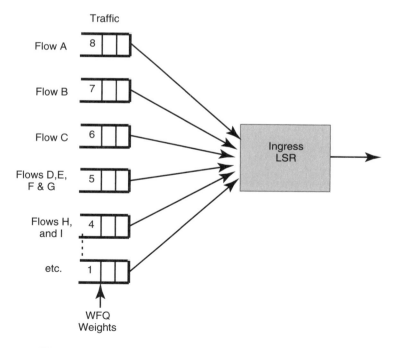

Figure 7–8   Multiple MPLS flows per traffic class.

SUMMARY

This chapter explained two aspects of MPLS: (a) how networks in general are engineered to provide efficient services to its customers, and (b) how MPLS plays a role in supporting these services. The importance of queue management was emphasized, and we examined several traffic engineering algorithms, with the emphasis on token buckets and WFQ.

8

MPLS and DiffServ

T his chapter explains how MPLS networks support differentiated services (DiffServ or DS) operations. It describes how DiffServ behavior aggregates (BAs) are mapped onto label switched paths (LSPs) in order to best match DiffServ traffic engineering and QOS objectives.

DIFFSERV CONCEPTS

The main ideas of Diffserv are to (a) classify traffic at the boundaries of network, and (b) regulate (condition) this traffic at the boundaries. The classification operation entails the assignment of the traffic to behavioral aggregates (BAs). These behavioral aggregates are a collection of packets with common characteristics, as far as how they are identified and treated by the network. The network classifies the packets based on the content of the packet headers. The idea is to have a small number of classifications to simplify the allocation of resources for the traffic classes.

The identified traffic is assigned a value, a differentiated services codepoint. For IPv4, the codepoint is the use of 6 bits of the TOS field; for IPv6, the codepoint is in the traffic class octet. Since DiffServ assumes the use of just a few traffic classes, the "redefined" TOS field is considered sufficient to handle the different classes (64 of them).

Per Hop Behavior

After the packets have been classified at the boundary of the network, they are forwarded through the network based on the DS codepoint (DSCP). The forwarding is performed on a per-hop basis; that is, the DS node alone decides how the forwarding is to be carried out. This concept is called *per-hop behavior* (PHB). At each node, the DSCP is used to select the PHB, which in turn determines the scheduling treatment for the packet, and possibly the drop probability for the packet.

THE DIFFSERV DOMAIN

Diffserv uses the idea of a DS domain, shown in Figure 8–1. A collection of networks operating under an administration could be a DS domain, say an ISP. It is responsible for meeting a service level agreement (SLA) between the user and the DS domain service provider.

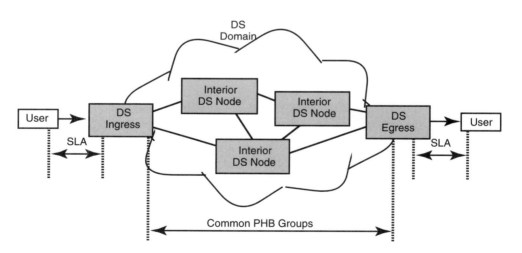

Where:
   DS: DiffServ
   PHB: per-hop behavior
   SLA: service level agreement

Figure 8–1   The DiffServ domain.

The DS domain consists of a contiguous set of nodes that are DS-compliant and agree to a common set of service provisioning policies. The DS domain also operates with a common per-hop behavior definition (more than one PHB is allowed and are called PHB groups). The PHB defines how a collection of packets with the same DS codepoint are treated.

The DS domain contains DS boundary nodes that are responsible for the classifying operations and the conditioning of ingress traffic. I will have more to say about conditioning later; for this introduction, it consists of controlling the traffic to make sure it "behaves" according to the rules of the DS domain (and, one hopes, the desires of the user).

Once past the ingress node and inside the DS domain, the internal nodes forward packets based on the DS codepoint. Their job is to map the DS codepoint value to a supported PHB. Thus, there are DS boundary nodes and DS interior nodes. The DS boundary nodes connect the DS domain to other DS domains or noncompliant systems. There is no restriction on what type of machine executes the boundary or interior node operations. For instance, a host might play the role of a DS boundary node.

TYPES OF PER-HOP BEHAVIORS

Three types of PHBs are defined in the DS specifications. DiffServ defines a default PHB in which there is no special treatment accorded to the packet. It also defines expedited forwarding (EF), a method in which certain packets are given low delay and low loss service. Typically, these packets are regulated such that their queues are serviced at a rate in which the packets are removed from the buffer at least as quickly as packets are placed into the buffer.

The third PHB definition is assured forwarding (AF) [HEIN99].[1] This PHB is a tool to offer different levels of forwarding assurances for IP packets received from a user. (The WFQ operations discussed in Chapter 7 would be good tools for managing AF traffic).

Four AF classes are defined, where each AF class in each DS node is allocated a certain amount of forwarding resources (buffer space and bandwidth). Within each AF, class packets are marked (again by the user or the service provider) with one of three possible drop precedence values. Thus, the number of AF PHBs is 12.

---

[1][HEIN99] Heinanen, J. et al., "Assured Forwarding PHB Group," RFC 2597, June 1999.

In case of congestion, the drop precedence of a packet determines the relative importance of the packet within the AF class. A congested DS node tries to protect packets with a lower drop precedence value from being lost by preferably discarding packets with a higher drop precedence value.

Within each AF class, an IP packet is assigned one of M different levels of drop precedence. A packet that belongs to an AF class i and has drop precedence j is marked with the AF codepoint AFij, where $1 <= i <= N$ and $1 <= j <= M$. Currently, four classes (N=4) with three levels of drop precedence in each class (M=3) are defined for general use.

Figure 8–2 shows how AF queues are set up at a DS LSR. The value i can be used to identify the queue for the packet, with each queue hold-

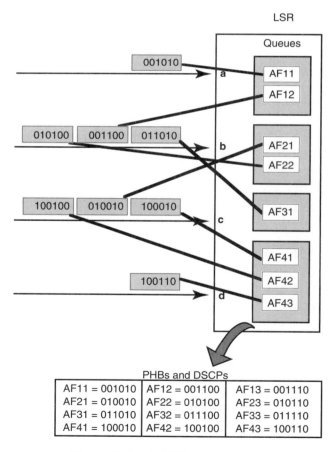

PHBs and DSCPs		
AF11 = 001010	AF12 = 001100	AF13 = 001110
AF21 = 010010	AF22 = 010100	AF23 = 010110
AF31 = 011010	AF32 = 011100	AF33 = 011110
AF41 = 100010	AF42 = 100100	AF43 = 100110

Figure 8–2   DSCPs and PHBs.

ing a class of traffic. The value j determines the drop preference of the packets belonging to the same queue. Four queues are set up at the DS LSR, and four incoming links are delivering packets across interfaces a, b, c, and d. The DSCPs in the packets are used to place the packets in their respective queues, and the AF PHB operations at this node determine how the packets are handled.

Note that the packets within each of the four queues are distinguished only by their drop preference. Of course, each queue is handled differently. Also, note that the table at the bottom of the figure is used at the LSR to correlate the DSCP to a PHB, thus determining how the packet is treated at the LSR.

MPLS AND DIFFSERV ROUTERS

Considerable work is going on in the Internet working groups to define the relationships between MPLS and DiffServ, and the emphasis in this chapter is on [LIWE00].[2] Recall that DiffServ redefines the IPv4 TOS field, and names it the DS codepoint. This field does not have to be processed by the MPLS transit routers, but it must be visible to the ingress and egress LSRs.

As shown in Figure 8–3, the egress router may use the DSCP to make decisions about how to code the MPLS label. Therefore, the label selection can determine how the traffic is treated in the network, if the DSCP is used to determine the label.

The format for the MPLS header is shown (again) in Figure 8–4. It consists of the following fields:

- *Label*: Label value, 20 bits. This value contains the MPLS label.
- *EXP*: Experimental use, 3 bits. This field is not yet fully defined. Several Internet working papers on DiffServ discuss its use with this specification.
- *S*: Stacking bit, 1 bit. Used to stack multiple labels, and discussed earlier in this book.
- *TTL*: Time to live, 8 bits. Places a limits on how many hops the MPLS PDU can traverse. This is needed because the IP TTL field is not examined by the transit LSRs.

---

[2][LIWE00] Liwen, Wu. et al., "MPLS Support of Differentiated Servies," *draft-ietf-mple-diff-ext-04.txt,* March 2000.

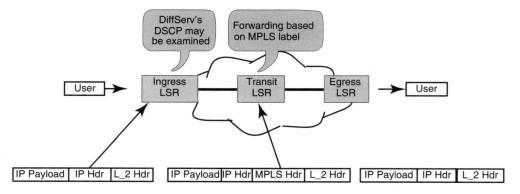

Where DSCP is the DiffServ Codepoint (residing in the IPv4 header).

Figure 8–3   MPLS and DiffServ.

TRAFFIC CLASSIFICATION AND CONDITIONING

The DS node must provide traffic classification and conditioning operations, as shown in Figure 8–5. The job of packet classification is to identify subsets of traffic that are to receive differentiated services by the DS domain. Classifiers operate in two modes: (a) the behavior aggregate classifier classifies packets only on the DS codepoint, (b) the multifield classifier classifies packets by multiple fields in the packet, such as codepoints, addresses, and port numbers. The BA defines all the traffic crossing a link that requires the same DS behavior.

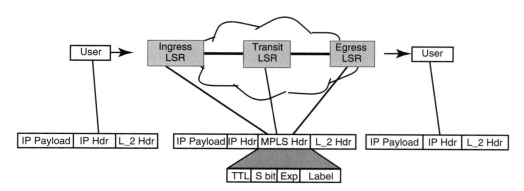

Figure 8–4   Format for the MPLS header.

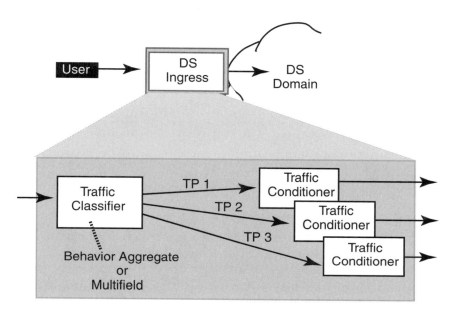

Note: Traffic classifiers can also be located at egress boundary nodes, or within the interior of the DS domain.

Where TP = traffic profile

Figure 8–5   DiffServ classifiers and conditioners.

The DS Classifiers

The classifiers provide the mechanism to guide the packets to a traffic conditioner for more processing. The traffic stream selected by the classifier is based on a specific set of traffic profiles, such as variable or constant bit rates, jitter, and delay.

The packets that are presented to a specific traffic conditioner constitute a traffic profile (TP) and may be in-profile or out-of-profile. In-profile means the packets are "conformant" to the user-network SLA. Out-of-profile packets are outside an SLA or, due to network behavior, arrive at the traffic conditioner at a rate that requires the conditioner to condition them (delay their delivery, drop them, etc.).

As a general practice, classification and conditioning operations take place at the network boundaries. Nothing precludes the internal nodes from invoking these operations, but their classification and conditioning operations are probably more limited than the boundary nodes.

Behavior Aggregates, Ordered Aggregates, and LSPs

The job of the MPLS network is to select how the DS BAs are mapped in the MPLS LSPs. In so doing, the network administrator must be aware of another DS concept: the ordered aggregate (OA). The OA is a set of BAs that share an ordering constraint.

This term encompasses a DS rule that states that packets belonging to the same flow cannot be misordered if they differ only in drop precedence; that is, they must maintain the same order from the ingress LSR to the egress LSR. The effect of this rule is that packets belonging to the same set, such as AF21, AF22, and so on, are placed in a common queue for FIFO operations.

This idea is quite similar to ATM and Frame Relay. They also require that cells or frames belonging to a single virtual circuit cannot be misordered as they transit an ATM or Frame Relay network.

DS also defines the set of one or more PHBs that are applied to this set. The result of this definition is called a PHB scheduling class (PSC). The network administrator must decide if the sets of BAs are mapped onto the same LSP or different LSPs in one of two ways.

- LSPs that can transport multiple ordered aggregates, so that the EXP field of the MPLS shim header conveys to the LSR the PHB to be applied to the packet (covering both information about the packet's scheduling treatment and its drop precedence).
- LSPs that transport only a single ordered aggregate, so that the packet's scheduling treatment is inferred by the LSR exclusively from the packet's label value, while the packet's drop precedence is conveyed in the EXP field of the MPLS shim header or in the encapsulating link layer-specific selective drop mechanism (ATM, Frame Relay).

Figure 8–6 shows a logical view of the relationships of the key DS functions for DS packet classification and traffic conditioning operations. The packets that exit the DS node in this figure must have the DS codepoint set to an appropriate value, based on the classification and traffic conditioning operations.

A traffic stream is selected by a classifier and sent to a traffic conditioner. DiffServ uses the term traffic conditioning block (TCB) to describe the overall conditioning operations. If appropriate, a meter is used to measure the traffic against a traffic profile. The results of the metering procedure may be used to mark, shape, or drop the traffic, based on the

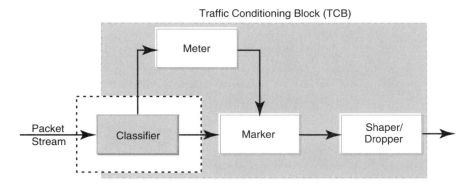

Figure 8–6   The DS traffic classification and conditioning model.

packet being in-profile or out-of-profile. The classifiers and meters can operate as a "team" to determine how the packet is treated with regard to marking, shaping, and dropping.

The packet marking procedure sets the DS field of a packet to a codepoint and adds the marked packet to a specific DS behavior aggregate. The marker can be configured to mark all packets steered to it to a single codepoint. Alternately, the marker can mark a packet to one of a set of codepoints. The idea of this configuration is to select a PHB in a PHB group, according to the state of a meter. The changing of the codepoint is called *packet remarking.*

The shaping procedure is used to bring the packet stream into compliance with a particular traffic profile. The packet stream is stored in the shaper's buffer, and a packet may be discarded if there is not enough buffer space to hold a delayed packet.

The dropping procedure polices the packet stream in order to bring it into conformance with a particular traffic profile. It can drop packets to adhere to the profile. The figure shows the shaper and dropper as one entity because a dropper can be implemented as a special case of a shaper.

The originating node of the packet stream (the DS source domain) is allowed to perform classification and conditioning operations. This idea is called premarking and can be effective in supporting the end application's view of the required QOS for the packet stream. The source node may mark the codepoint to indicate high-priority traffic. Next, a first-hop router may mark this traffic with another codepoint, and condition the packet stream.

I stated that the collective operations of metering, marking, shaping, and dropping are known as the traffic conditioning block. The classi-

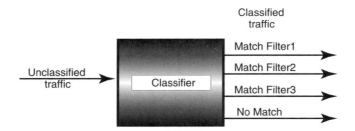

Figure 8–7   Example of the classifier's filtering operations.

fier need not be a part of the TCB, because it does not condition traffic. However, the classifiers and traffic conditioners can certainly be combined into the TCB. These options are shown in Figure 8–6 with the dashed lines.

The next part of this chapter goes into more detail on the classifiers and traffic conditioners. This material is available from the Internet draft authored by [BERN99].[3]

CLASSIFICATION OPERATIONS

The main job of the classifier is to accept a packet stream (unclassified traffic) as input and generate separate output streams (classified traffic). This output is fed into the metering or marking functions.

As mentioned earlier, the classifier operates as a behavior aggregate classifier or as a multifield (MF) classifier. The BA classifier uses only the DS codepoint to sort to an output stream, whereas the MF classifier uses other fields in the packet stream, such as a port number or an IP Protocol ID.

The BA or MF classifier checks are performed by filters, which are a set of conditions that are matched to the relevant fields in the packet to determine onto which output stream the packet is placed. This idea is shown in Figure 8–7. Unclassified traffic is flowing into an interface and passed to the classifier. The filtering operations output the packets into four streams for the traffic conditioning operations. The first three filters are exact matches on the BA or MA values. The no-match is a default filter to handle any packet types that have not been provisioned at the QOS node.

---

[3][BERN99] Bernet, Y., et al., "A Conceptual Model for DiffServ Routers," *draft-ietf-fiddserv-model-00.txt,* June 1999.

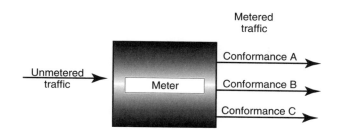

Figure 8–8   Example of the metering operations.

METERING OPERATIONS

After the packets have been classified, the meter monitors their arrival time in the packet stream to determine the level of conformance to a traffic profile. The profile has been preconfigured, perhaps based on an SLA contract.

Figure 8–8 is a functional diagram of the metering operation. The unmetered traffic is input to the metering function. This function is implemented with one or several types of meters defined in [BERN99], but others can be used: (a) the average rate meter, (b) the exponential weighted moving average meter, (c) the token bucket meter. These meters are explained in Chapter 7.

THE DS CODEPOINT REVISITED

As explained earlier, the DS field in the IP datagram is the IPv4 TOS field. It is called the DS codepoint (DSCP). This IPv4 8-bit field is shown in Figure 8–9, along with the redefinition according to the DS specifications.

The IPv4 *type of service (TOS)* field, shown in Figure 8–9(a), can be used to identify several QOS functions provided for an Internet application. Transit delay, throughput, precedence, and reliability can be requested with this field.

The TOS field contains five entries, consisting of 8 bits. Bits 0, 1, and 2 contain a precedence value which is used to indicate the relative importance of the datagram. The next three bits are used for other services and are described as follows: Bit 3 is the *delay bit (D bit)*. When set to 1, this TOS requests a short delay through an internet. The aspect of delay is not defined in the standard and it is up to the vendor to imple-

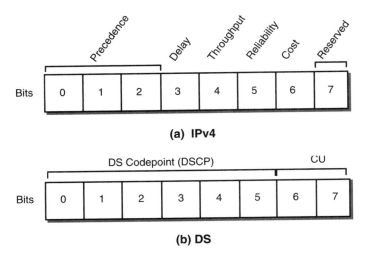

Figure 8–9   The IPv4 TOS field and the DS codepoint.

ment the service. The next bit is the *throughput bit (T bit)*. It is set to 1 to request for high throughput through an internet. Again, its specific implementation is not defined in the standard. The next bit used is the *reliability bit (R bit)*, which allows a user to request high reliability for the datagram. The last bit of interest is the *cost bit (C bit)*, which is set to request the use of a low-cost link (from the standpoint of monetary cost). The last bit is not used at this time.

The DSCP is six bits in length, as depicted in Figure 8–9(b). The remaining two bits of the TOS field are currently unused (CU). The DSCP notation is xxxxxx, where x may be a 1 or 0. The left-most bit signifies bit 0 of the field, and the right-most bit signifies bit 5. The entire 6-bit field is used by DS nodes as an index into a table to select a specific packet-handling mechanism.

The codepoints are related to the PHBs, and the PHBs include a default codepoint. A default configuration contains a recommended codepoint-to-PHB mapping. The default PHB is the conventional best-effort forwarding operation that exists today and is standardized in RFC 1812. When a link is not needed to satisfy another PHB, the traffic associated with the default PHB should be placed onto the link. RFC 2474 states that a default PHB should not be subject to bandwidth starvation and should be given some bandwidth, but the manner in which the bandwidth is provided is implementation-specific. The available bit rate (ABR) operation in ATM is a good model to use for this implementation. The default codepoint for the default PHB is 000000.

Table 8–1   Recommended AF Code Points and AF Classes

	Class 1	Class 2	Class 3	Class 4
Low Drop Prec	001010	010010	011010	100010
Medium Drop Prec	001100	010100	011100	100100
High Drop Prec	001110	010110	011110	100110

The recommended codepoints may be amended or replaced with different codepoints, at the discretion of the service provider. Even if the same PHBs are implemented on both sides of a DS boundary, the DSCP still may be remarked.

If a DS node receives a packet containing an unrecognized codepoint, it simply treats the packet as if it were marked with the default codepoint. This rule means the DS node may examine other fields in the IP header (or layer 4 header) in order to know about the default codepoint. I make this point because this rule implies that a DS node must be able to review fields other than the codepoint. Strictly speaking, the fewer fields examined the better. If only the codepoint is examined, the operation can be very efficient, similar to ATM label switching.

The DSCP field can convey 64 distinct codepoints, as depicted in Table 8–1 and Figure 8–2. The codepoint space is divided into three pools for the purpose of codepoint assignment and management.

A pool of 32 codepoints (Pool 1) is assigned by Standards Action as defined in the ongoing Internet standards. See Table 8–2. A pool of 16 codepoints (Pool 2) is reserved for experimental or local use (EXP/LU), and a pool of 16 codepoints (Pool 3) which are initially available for experimental or local use. The DS standards state that pool 3 should be preferentially utilized for standardized assignments if Pool 1 is exhausted.

Table 8–2   Codepoint Assignments

Pool	Codepoint Space	Assignment Policy
1	xxxxx0	Standards Action
2	xxxx11	EXP/LU
3	xxxx01	EXP/LU (*)

(*) may be utilized for future allocations as necessary

Code Points for Assured Forwarding

The recommended codepoints for the four general use assured forwarding (AF) classes are listed below and in Figure 8–2. These codepoints do not overlap with any other general use PHB groups.

AF11 = 001010, AF12 = 001100, AF13 = 001110,
AF21 = 010010, AF22 = 010100, AF23 = 010110,
AF31 = 011010, AF32 = 011100, AF33 = 011110,
AF41 = 100010, AF42 = 100100, AF43 = 100110

DSCPS AND LSR USE OF MPLS LABELS

Recall that an interior LSR does not examine the IP header. The ingress LSR may examine the IP header for information to create an LSP and associated labels. Some means must be available to correlate the DS PHB with the packet. At first glance, it seems an easy task. Simply map the information in the DSCP into the label and or the EXP fields of the shim header. It is not quite so straightforward, and this part of the chapter explains why.

The DSCP in the TOS field is 6 bits in length, and the EXP field in the MPLS shim header is 3 bits in length. Early in the development of DiffServ, it was intended that the 3-bit EXP field would support DS operations. The obvious problem is that the number of bits in these fields differ. This situation occurred because the EXP field was defined before the DiffServ working group was set up, and it was believed that 3 bits would suffice. In addition, the old precedence field (also 3 bits in length) had been the field that routers used for making QOS decisions.[4]

In addition, some designers think eight classes of traffic is sufficient to provide enough granularity for effective QOS operations. For that matter, a number of systems support only two classes of traffic, similar to the EF PHBs.

Moreover, as with any field, the working group wished to keep the shim header small, and eight classes of traffic seemed appropriate. But, as noted in the previous discussion, the 6-bit DSCP allows for up to 64 DSCPs.

Certainly, if a network supports eight or fewer PHBs, there is no problem. Let's assume a router is configured to support both MPLS and

---

[4]The TOS field is still in use for QOS functions. For example, the Cisco router defines several procedures for prioritization of traffic by the use of this field, a topic explained in Chapter 7.

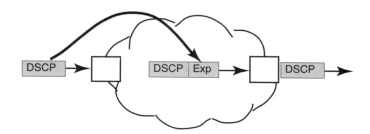

Figure 8–10   Mapping DSCP and EXP values to PHBs.

DiffServ operations. The following holds: (a) the DS-LSR maps DSCP values to suitable PHBs, and (b) the DS-LSR maps EXP values to suitable PHBs, a process depicted in Figure 8–10.

THE ORDERED AGGREGATE AND MPLS LSPs

Recall that an OA is a set of BAs that share an ordering constraint, and DS can define the set of one or more PHBs that are applied to this set. This ordering constraint has an interesting effect on MPLS LSPs. Since AF packets of the same class (say AF21, AF22, etc.) must not be misordered, they should be assigned to the same LSP.

The result of this situation is the PHB scheduling class: a group of packets belonging to the same PHB must be sent over the same LSP. Two aspects of the PSC are of interest here: (a) the EXP-inferred-PSC LSPs, and (b) the label-only-inferred-PSC LSPs. Let's take a look at these operations.

EXP-Inferred-PSC LSPs

By using the 3-bit EXP field, a single LSP can be used to support up to eight BAs of a given FEC. These LSPs are called EXP-inferred-PSC LSPs (E-LSP), since the PSC of a packet transported on this LSP depends on the EXP field value for the packet. With this approach, the label can be used by the router to make forwarding decisions, and the EXP filed can be used to determine how to treat the packet.

Label-Only-Inferred-PSC LSPs

A separate LSP can be established for a single <FEC, OA> pair. With such LSPs, the PSC is explicitly signaled at label establishment time so that after label establishment, the LSR can infer exclusively from the label value the PSC to be applied to a labeled packet. This approach, inferring forwarding and ordering from the label, is a common implementation in ATM and Frame Relay networks.

When the shim header is used, the drop precedence to be applied by the LSR to the labeled packet is conveyed inside the labeled packet MPLS shim header using the EXP field. When the shim header is not used (such as MPLS over ATM or Frame Relay), the drop precedence is conveyed inside the link layer header encapsulation, using link layer-specific drop precedence fields (e.g., the ATM cell loss priority (CLP) bit or the Frame Relay discard eligibility (DE) bit).

This approach is called label-only-inferred-PSC LSPs (L-LSP) because the PSC can be inferred from the label without any other information (e.g., regardless of the EXP value).

Bandwidth Reservations for E-LSPs and L-LSPs

The Working Group defining MPLS support of DiffServ has developed the following guidelines for bandwidth reservations for E-LSPs and L-LSPs [FAUC00].[5]

E-LSPs and L-LSPs may be established with or without bandwidth reservation. Establishing an E-LSP or L-LSP with bandwidth reservation means that bandwidth requirements for the LSP are signaled at LSP establishment time. Such signaled bandwidth requirements may be used by LSRs at establishment time to perform admission control of the signaled LSP over the DiffServ resources provisioned for the relevant PSC(s). Such signaled bandwidth requirements may also be used by LSRs at establishment time to perform adjustment to the DiffServ resources associated with the relevant PSC(s), for example, to adjust PSC scheduling weight.

When bandwidth requirements are signaled during the establishment of an L-LSP, the signaled bandwidth is obviously associated with the L-LSP's PSC. Thus, LSRs that use the signaled bandwidth to perform admission control may perform admission control over DiffServ resources that are dedicated to the PSC, for example, over the bandwidth guaranteed to the PSC through its scheduling weight.

When bandwidth requirements are signaled at establishment of an E-LSP, the signaled bandwidth is associated collectively to the whole LSP and therefore to the set of transported PSCs. Thus, LSRs that use

---

[5][FAUC00] Le Faucheur, Francois et al., "MPLS Support of Differentiated Services," *draft-ietf-mpls-diff-ext-04.txt,* March 2000.

the signaled bandwidth to perform admission control may perform admission control over global resources which are shared by the set of PSCs (e.g., over the total bandwidth of the link).

SUMMARY

In this chapter, we learned how MPLS networks support differentiated services (DiffServ or DS) operations. We also examined how DiffServ behavior aggregates are mapped onto label switched paths in order to best match DiffServ traffic engineering and QOS objectives.

9

Constraint-Based Routing

This chapter explains a traffic engineering function called constraint-based routing. The primary focus is on how LSPs are established with LDP, but other alternatives such as a modified OSPF and RSVP are discussed. Earlier chapters explained some of the basic and MPLS-oriented features of RSVP, and you may wish to review this material before reading the section on RSVP.

The information in this chapter is based on the MPLS working drafts, and especially on [JAMO99],[1] and several papers from [FORO00].[2] Be aware that this information is closely tied to the traffic engineering discussions in Chapter 7, which is prerequisite reading. In addition, constraint-based routing is explained in relation to ATM, Frame Relay, and RSVP in Appendix B.

THE BASIC CONCEPT

Constraint-based routing (CR) is a mechanism used to meet traffic engineering requirements for MPLS networks. The basic concept is to extend LDP for support of constraint-based routed label switched paths

---

[1][JAMO99] Jamoussi, Bilel. "Constraint-Based LSP Setup Using LDP," *draft-ietf-mpls-cr-ldp-03.txt,* September 1999.
[2][FORO00] MPLS Forum 2000 Conference, 7–10 March 2000, Hotel Sofitel, Rive Gauche, France.

(CR-LSPs) by defining mechanisms and additional type-length-values (TLVs) for support of CR-LSPs, or to use existing protocols to support constraint-based routing.

CR can be set up as an end-to-end operation; that is, from the ingress CR-LSR to the egress CR-LSR. The idea is for the ingress CR-LSR to initiate CR and for all affected nodes to be able to reserve resources using LDP.

The term *constraint* is used to imply that in a network, and for each set of nodes, there exists a set of constraints that must be satisfied for the link or links between the two nodes. An example of a constraint is a path that has a minimum amount of bandwidth. Another example is a path that is secure. The protocol that finds such paths (such as a modified OSPF) is constrained to advertise (and find) paths in the routing domain that satisfy these kinds of constraints.

In addition, constraint-based routing attempts to meet a set of constraints, and at the same time, optimize some scalar metric [DAVI00].[3] One important scalar metric is hop-count for delay-sensitive traffic. Experience has shown that extra hops create jitter, especially if the Internet is busy and the routers are processing a lot of traffic.

EXPLICIT ROUTING

Explicit routing (ER) is integral to constraint-based routing. This route is set up at the edge of the network, based on QOS criteria and routing information. Figure 9–1 shows an example of explicit routing.

The explicit route starts at ingress router A and traverses B, then D, and exits at egress router F. The explicit route is not allowed to traverse LSRs C and E. The allowed route can be established by using LDP messages. Based on [JAMO99],[4] the explicit route is coded in a label request message. The message contains a list of nodes (or group of nodes) that define the CR route. After the CR-LSP has been established, all of a subset of the nodes in a group can be traversed by the LSP.

The capability to specify groups of nodes, of which a subset will be traversed by the CR-LSP, allows the system a significant amount of local flexibility in fulfilling a request for a constraint-based route. Moreover,

---

[3][DAVI00] Davie, Bruce and Rekhter, Yakov, *MPLS: Technology and Applications,* San Diego: Academic Press, 2000.

[4][JAMO99] Jamoussi, Belel et. al., "Constraint-Based LSP Setup Using LDP," *draft-ietf-mpla-cr-ldp-03.txt,* September 1999.

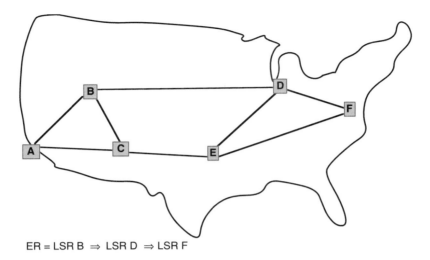

ER = LSR B ⇒ LSR D ⇒ LSR F

Figure 9–1   Explicit routing.

constraint-based routing requires the path to be calculated by the source of the LSP traffic.

LDP and Constraint-based Routing

If LDP is used for constraint-based routing, the constraint-based route is encoded as a series of ER-hops contained in a constraint-based route TLV, explained later in this chapter. Each ER-hop may identify a group of nodes in the constraint-based route, and TLVs are available that describe traffic parameters, such as peak rate and committed rate. A constraint-based route is then a path including all of the identified groups of nodes in the order in which they appear in the TLV.

PRE-EMPTION

CR-LDP conveys the resources required by a path on each hop of the route. If a route with sufficient resources cannot be found, existing paths may be rerouted to reallocate resources to the new path. For example, in Figure 9–1, if node B is down or has insufficient resources to meet the QOS requirements of the FEC, node C can be selected instead.

This idea is called *path pre-emption*. Setup and holding priorities are used to rank existing paths (holding priority) and the new path (setup priority) to determine if the new path can preempt an existing path.

The setup priority of a new CR-LSP and the holding priority attributes of the existing CR-LSP are used to specify priorities. Signaling a higher holding priority expresses that the path, once it has been established, should have a lower chance of being preempted. Signaling a higher setup priority expresses the expectation that, in the case that resources are unavailable, the path is more likely to preempt other paths. The setup and holding priority values range from 0 to 7. The value 0 is the priority assigned to the most important path. It is referred to as the highest priority. The value 7 is the priority for the least important path.

The setup priority of a CR-LSP should not be higher (numerically less) than its holding priority since it might bump an LSP and be bumped by the next equivalent request.

THE CR MESSAGES AND TLVS

This part of the chapter describes the CR messages and TLVs. The contents and general purpose of each message is explained, and in subsequent sections of the chapter, more details are provided.

Label Request Message

The Label Request message is modified from LDP, and shown in Figure 9–2. Several fields in this message have been explained in Chapter 5. The new TLVs are examined in the next section of this chapter.

Label Mapping Message

The Label Mapping message is shown in Figure 9–3. This message is sent by a downstream LSR to an upstream LSR if one of these conditions has been satisfied: (a) the LSR is the egress end of the CR-LSP, and an upstream mapping has been requested, (b) the LSR received a mapping from its downstream next hop LSR for a CR-LSR for which an upstream request is still pending.

Notification Message

Notification messages, shown in Figure 9–4, carry status TLVs to specify events being signaled. Notification messages are forwarded toward the LSR originating the label request at each hop.

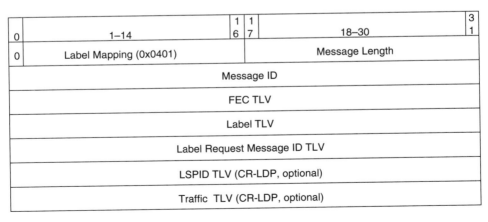

0	1–14	1 6	1 7	18–30	3 1
0	Label Request (0x0401)			Message Length	
	Message ID				
	FEC TLV				
	LSPID TLV (CR-LDP, mandatory)				
	ER-TLV (CR-LDP, optional)				
	Traffic TLV (CR-LDP, optional)				
	Pinning TLV (CR-LDP, optional)				
	Resource Class TV (CR-LDP, optional)				
	Pre-emption TLV (CR-LDP, optional)				

Figure 9–2   The Label Request message.

Explicit Route TLV

The explicit route TLV, depicted in Figure 9–5, specifies the path to be taken by the LSP that is being established. It contains one or more explicit hop TLVs, explained next.

Explicit Route Hop TLV

The explicit route hop TLV contains the hop identifiers. The TLV is shown in Figure 9–6. The ER-Hop-Type field conveys information about

0	1–14	1 6	1 7	18–30	3 1
0	Label Mapping (0x0401)			Message Length	
	Message ID				
	FEC TLV				
	Label TLV				
	Label Request Message ID TLV				
	LSPID TLV (CR-LDP, optional)				
	Traffic TLV (CR-LDP, optional)				

Figure 9–3   Label Mapping message.

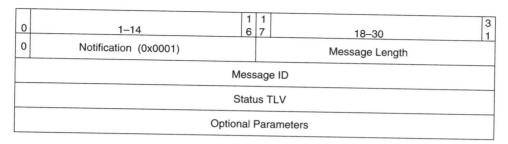

0		1–14		1 6	1 7		18–30		3 1
0		Notification (0x0001)					Message Length		
				Message ID					
				Status TLV					
				Optional Parameters					

Figure 9–4   Notification message.

the contents field, indicating this field is IPv4 prefix, IPv6 prefix, autonomous system (AS) number, or an LSPID. The L bit indicates if the node or group operates as loose or strict routing. The content field contains the prefixes, or whatever is being conveyed in this TLV.

Traffic Parameters TLV

Figure 9–7 shows the format for the traffic parameter TLV. As the name implies, it is used to convey traffic parameters to other CR-LSR nodes. The fields in the TLV perform the following functions. Please note that the traffic engineering parameters of peak rate through excess burst size are explained in the chapter on traffic engineering (Chapter 7, see section, "Constraint-based Routing as Defined by the IETF").

The flag field performs a number of functions. The first two bits are reserved for future use. The remaining six bits are defined as follows. Each flag bit is a negotiable flag corresponding to a traffic parameter. The negotiable flag value 0 denotes not negotiable and value 1 denotes negotiable.

0	1	2–14		1 6	1 7		18–30		3 1
0	0	ER-TLV (0x0800)					Length		
				ER-Hop 1					
				ER-Hop 2					
				ER-Hop n					

Figure 9–5   Explicit route TLV.

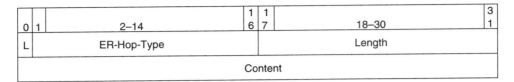

0	1	2–14	1 6	1 7	18–30	3 1
L		ER-Hop-Type			Length	
Content						

Figure 9–6   The explicit route hop TLV.

F1 - Corresponds to the PDR.
F2 - Corresponds to the PBS.
F4 - Corresponds to the CBS.
F5 - Corresponds to the EBS.
F6 - Corresponds to the Weight.

The frequency field is coded with the following code points defined:

0- Unspecified
1- Frequent
2- Very frequent
3–255 - Reserved

The weight field indicates the weight of the CR-LSP. Valid weight values are from 1 to 255. The value 0 means that weight is not applicable for the CR-LSP.

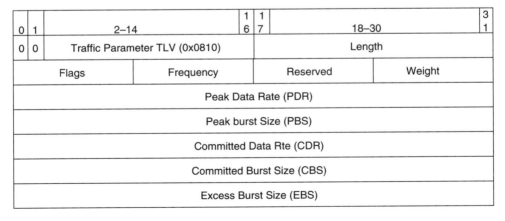

Figure 9–7   The traffic parameters TLV.

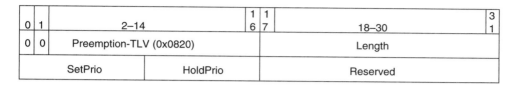

0	1	2–14	1 6	1 7	18–30	3 1
0	0	Preemption-TLV (0x0820)			Length	
	SetPrio		HoldPrio		Reserved	

Figure 9–8   The preemption TLV.

Each Traffic Parameter is encoded as a 32-bit number. The values PDR and CDR are in units of bytes-per-second. The values PBS, CBS, and EBS are in units of bytes. Once again, these traffic parameters are explained in Chapter 7.

Pre-emption TLV

The preemption TLV is shown in Figure 9–8. The two key fields in the TLV are SetPrio (SetupPriority) and HoldPrio (HoldingPriority). A SetupPriority of 0 is the priority assigned to the most important path. It is referred to as the highest priority. Seven (7) is the priority for the least important path.

A HoldingPriority of 0 is the priority assigned to the most important path. It is referred to as the highest priority. Seven (7) is the priority for the least important path.

LSPID TLV

The LSPID TLV is shown in Figure 9–9. It is a unique ID of a CR-LSP. The LSPID is composed of the ingress LSR Router ID (or any of its own Ipv4 addresses) and a locally unique CR-LSP ID to that LSR. The LSPID is useful in network management, in CR-LSP repair, and in using an already established CR-LSP as a hop in an ER-TLV.

An action indicator flag is carried in the LSPID TLV, and indicates explicitly the action that should be taken if the LSP already exists on the LSR receiving the message.

0	1	2–10	1 1	1 2	13 –14	1 5	1 6	17–30	3 1
0	0	LSPID-TLV (0x0821)						Length	
Reserved				Act Flg				Local CR-LSP ID	
Ingress LSR Router ID									

Figure 9–9   LSPID TLV.

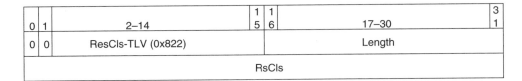

Figure 9–10   Resource class TLV.

After a CR-LSP is set up, its bandwidth reservation may need to be changed by the network provider, due to the new requirements for the traffic carried on that CR-LSP. The _action indicator flag_ is used to indicate the need to modify the bandwidth and possibly other parameters of an established CR-LSP without service interruption.

The Local LSP ID is an identifier of the CR-LSP locally unique within the ingress LSR originating the CR-LSP. The ingress LSR Router ID simply identifies the ingress LSR router.

Resource Class TLV

The resource class TLV, shown in Figure 9–10, is used to specify which links are acceptable by this CR-LSP and to prune the topology of the network. The RsCLs field (resource class bit mask) indicates which of the 32 nodes the CR-LSP can traverse.

Route Pinning TLV

Figure 9–11 shows the TLV format for route pinning. Route pinning is applicable to segments of an LSP that are loosely routed—i.e., those segments that are specified with a next hop with the L bit set or where the next hop is an _abstract node_. A CR-LSP may be set up using route pinning if it is undesirable to change the path used by an LSP even when a better next hop becomes available at some LSR along the loosely routed portion of the LSP.

The P bit is set to 1 to indicate that route pinning is requested. The P bit is set to 0 to indicate that route pinning is not requested.

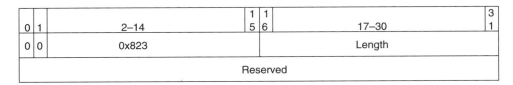

Figure 9–11   The route pinning TLV.

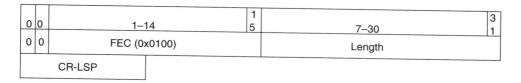

Figure 9–12   The CR-LSP FEC TLV.

CR-LSP FEC TLV

A new FEC element, shown in Figure 9–12, supports CR-LSPs. It does not preclude the use of other FECs elements (Type=0x01, 0x02, 0x03) defined in the LDP spec in CR-LDP messages. The CR-LDP FEC element is an opaque FEC to be used only in messages of CR-LSPs.

SUMMARY

This chapter explained a traffic engineering function called constraint-based routing. The primary focus was on how LSPs are established with LDP. The basic idea of constraint-based routing is to meet the traffic engineering requirements for MPLS networks. Indeed, constraint-based routing is closely associated with the traffic engineering concepts explained in Chapter 7.

10

Other Key Concepts of MPLS

This chapter contains information on other key concepts of MPLS networks that do not fit neatly into the other chapters. Summaries of several Internet Working Drafts are provided here, principally from [ROSE00, [ROSE99a], [NAGA00], [ANDE99],[1] and [BONI99].[2]

DETERMINING THE NETWORK LAYER PROTOCOL

In earlier chapters, we learned that when the packet reaches the egress LSR, no further label processing is performed; rather, the encapsulated network layer header is used to route the packet to its final destination.

The LSR that pops the last label off the stack must be able to identify the packet's network layer protocol. Since the label stack does not contain any field that explicitly identifies the network layer protocol, the identity of the network layer protocol is ascertained from the value of the

---

[1][ANDE99] Anderson, Loa et. al., "MPLS Capability Set," *draft-loa-mpls-cap-set-01.txt,* October 1999.

[2][BONI99] Bonica, R. et. al., "ICMP Extensions for MultiProtocol Label Switching," *draft-ietf-mpls-icmp-01.txt,* December 1999.

label that is popped from the bottom of the stack, possibly along with the contents of the network layer header itself.

In order for the final-popping LSR to know which network layer protocol it is to process, when the first label is pushed onto a network layer packet, either the label must be one which is used only for packets of a particular network layer, or the label must be one which is use only for a specified set of network layer protocols, where packets of the specified network layers can be distinguished by inspection of the network layer header.

GENERATING ICMP MESSAGES FOR LABELED IP PACKETS

It may be desirable to generate ICMP messages for labeled IP packets. If so, the MPLS requires two conditions to hold:

- It must be possible for that LSR to determine that a particular labeled packet is an IP packet.
- It must be possible for that LSR to route to the packet's IP source address.

PROCESSING THE TIME TO LIVE FIELD

The time to live (TTL) field plays a key role in internets to preclude an IP datagram from staying in existence too long. For MPLS, these rules are in effect. The *incoming TTL* of a labeled packet is defined to be the value of the TTL field of the top label stack entry when the packet is received.

The *outgoing TTL* of a labeled packet is defined to be the larger of (a) one less than the incoming TTL, or (b) zero.

If the outgoing TTL of a labeled packet is 0, then the labeled packet must not be further forwarded; nor may the label stack be stripped off and the packet forwarded as an unlabeled packet. The packet's lifetime in the network is considered to have expired.

Depending on the label value in the label stack entry, the packet may be simply discarded, or it may be passed to the appropriate "ordinary" network layer for error processing.

When a labeled packet is forwarded, the TTL field of the label stack entry at the top of the label stack *must* be set to the outgoing TTL value.

The outgoing TTL value is a function solely of the incoming TTL value and is independent of whether any labels are pushed or popped before forwarding. There is no significance to the value of the TTL field in any label stack entry that is not at the top of the stack.

When an IP packet is first labeled, the TTL field of the label stack entry must be set to the value of the IP TTL field. (If the IP TTL field needs to be decremented as part of the IP processing, it is assumed that this has already been done.)

When a label is popped and the resulting label stack is empty, then the value of the IP TTL field should be replaced with the outgoing TTL value, as defined above. In IPv4, this also requires modification of the IP header checksum.

FRAGMENTATION AND PATH MTU DISCOVERY

Just as it is possible to receive an unlabeled IP datagram that is too large to be transmitted on its output link, it is possible to receive a labeled packet that is too large to be transmitted on its output link.

It is also possible that a received packet (labeled or unlabeled), which was originally small enough to be transmitted on that link, becomes too large by virtue of having one or more additional labels pushed onto its label stack. In label switching, a packet may grow in size if additional labels get pushed on. Thus, if a labeled packet with a 1500-byte frame payload is received and an additional label is pushed onto it, it must be forwarded as a frame with a 1504-byte payload.

In general, IPv4 hosts that do not implement Path MTU Discovery send IP datagrams that contain no more than 576 bytes. Since the MTUs in use on most data links today are 1500 bytes or more, the probability that such datagrams will need to get fragmented, even if they get labeled, is very small.

Some hosts that do not implement Path MTU Discovery will generate IP datagrams containing 1500 bytes, as long as the IP source and destination addresses are on the same subnet. These datagrams will not pass through routers, and hence will not get fragmented.

Some hosts will generate IP datagrams containing 1500 bytes, as long the IP source and destination addresses have the same classful network number. This is the one case in which there is any risk of fragmentation when such datagrams get labeled.

CAPABILITY SETS

Several protocols might be used for label distribution in an MPLS network, for example, Label Distribution Protocol (LDP), including the part of LDP described in constraint-based LSP setup using LDP, the BGP-4 and RSVP.

The functionality defined in those protocols are to some extent overlapping, but also complementary. [ANDE99]specifies a number of MPLS capability sets that can be used to define what is needed from an MPLS implementation in order to interwork with other implementations. The number of capability sets might change in the future.

It has been noted that the functionality supported by most of the specifications on label distribution are richer than necessary for most applications. MPLS implementations implementing parts of one specification or a mix of parts from several specifications will be viable.

As all implementations won't support all of the specified mechanisms for label distribution specified in the MPLS standard, a tool for describing the compliance between MPLS implementations is required.

The following functional and protocol components are available in the protocols developed for and/or extended to do label distribution. All the specification listed below are worked on by the MPLS WG, and is still work in progress.

1. Carrying Label Information in BGP-4

   Defines mechanisms for:
   - assigning labels to BGP routes

2. Constraint based routing with LDP (CR-LDP)

   Defines mechanisms for:
   - explicit routed LSPs
   - LSP set up with defined QoS

3. Label Distribution Protocol (LDP)

   Defines mechanisms for:
   - basic LDP mechanisms
     - LDP neighbor detection

- LDP session initiation, maintenance and termination
- loop detection
- modes of label distribution defined in
  - Downstream Unsolicited Independent Control
  - Downstream Unsolicited Ordered Control
  - Downstream On Demand Independent Control
  - Downstream On Demand Ordered Control

4. Extensions to RSVP for LSP Tunnels

Defines mechanisms for:
- explicit routed LSPs
- dynamic distribution of labels (hop-by-hop mechanism)

Defined MPLS Capability Set

An MPLS Capability set defines the set of components that has to be supported by an implementation claiming compatibility with the capability set. Currently there are 10 Capability sets defined. Although there sometimes/frequently is an obviously a relationship between the Capability set and an intended use, this draft doesn't state the intended use of or the application possible to support by the capability set.

The intention is instead to give a reference framework that offers a possibility to classify compatibility of MPLS implementations. The Capability sets is atomic, i.e. it is not possible for an application to be compliant to part of a capability set. However it is possible for an application to be compliant with one or more capability sets.

Examples of Capability Sets

MPLS Capability set #1*

MPLS Capability set #1 includes the following components:

- LDP basic mechanisms
  - LDP neighbor detection
  - LDP session initiation, maintenance and termination
- CR-LDP strict explicit routed LSPs

This Capability set supports explicit routed LSP set up, but does not allow loosely routed segments on an explicit route. Note that this capability set do not require the loop detection mechanism.

MPLS Capability set #2

MPLS Capability set #2 includes the following components:

- LDP basic mechanisms
- CR-LDP explicit routed LSPs
- modes of label distribution defined in [5]
    - Downstream On Demand Ordered Control

This Capability set supports explicit routing and allows loosely routed segments of an explicit route.

MPLS Capability set #3

MPLS Capability set #3 includes the following components:

- LDP basic mechanisms
- CR-LDP explicit routed LSPs
- CR-LDP LSP set up with QoS
- modes of label distribution defined in [5]
    - Downstream On Demand Ordered Control

This Capability set supports explicit routing and allows loosely routed segments of an explicit route.

USE OF ICMP IN MPLS NETWORKS

This information is from [BONI95]:

MPLS Label Switching Routers (LSR) also use ICMP to convey control information to source hosts.

When an LSR receives an undeliverable MPLS encapsulated datagram, it removes the entire MPLS label stack, exposing the previously encapsulated IP datagram. The LSR then submits the IP datagram to a network-forwarding module for error processing. Error processing can include ICMP message generation.

The ICMP message indicates why the original datagram could not be delivered. It also contains the IP header and leading octets of the original datagram.

The ICMP message, however, includes no information regarding the MPLS label stack that encapsulated the original datagram when it arrived at the LSR. This omission is significant because the LSR would have routed the original datagram based upon information contained by the MPLS label stack.

The current memo proposes extensions to ICMP that permit an LSR to append MPLS label stack information to ICMP messages. ICMP messages regarding MPLS encapsulated datagrams SHOULD include the MPLS label stack, as it arrived at the router that is sending the ICMP message. The ICMP message MUST also include the IP header and leading payload octets of the original datagram.

SUMMARY

This chapter provided a brief and general description of several key concepts of MPCS Networks, with the emphasis on Capability Sets and ICMP. You should study [ANDE99] and [BONI99] for the detailed rules for these

Appendix A

Names, Addresses, Subnetting, Address Masks, and Prefixes

A newcomer to data networks is often perplexed when the subject of naming and addressing arises. Addresses in data networks are similar to postal addresses and telephone numbering schemes. Indeed, many of the networks that exist today have derived some of their addressing structures from the concepts of the telephone numbering plan.

It should prove useful to clarify the meaning of names, addresses, and routes. Table A–1 provides a summary of these ideas. A *name* is an identification of an entity (independent of its physical location), such as a person, an applications program, or even a computer. An *address* is also an identification, but it reveals additional information about the entity, principally information about its physical or logical placement in a network. A *route* is information on how to relay traffic to a physical location (address).

A network usually provides a service that allows a network user to furnish the network with a name of something (another user, an application, etc.) that is to receive traffic. A network *name server* then uses this name to determine the address of the receiving entity. This address is then used by a routing protocol to determine the physical route to the receiver.

With this approach, a network user does not become involved with and is not aware of physical addresses and the physical location of other

Table A–1   Names, Addresses, and Routes

Name An id of an entity, independent of physical location
    Example: JBrown@acme.com
Address An id that reveals a location of an entity
    Example: Network = 12.3, Subnetwork = 456, Host = 14
Route How to reach the entity at the address
    Example: Next node is Subnet 456
Practice is Name and address are correlated:
    12.3.456.14 is acme.com

users and network resources. This practice allows the network administrator to relocate and reconfigure network resources without affecting end users. Likewise, users can move to other physical locations, but their names remain the same. The network changes its naming/routing tables to reflect the relocation.

PRINCIPAL ADDRESSES USED IN INTERNET AND INTRANETS

Communications between users through a data network require several forms of addressing. Typically, two addresses are required: (a) a physical address, also called a data link address, or a media access control (MAC) address on a LAN, and (b) a network address. Other identifiers, such as upper layer names and/or port addresses, are needed for unambiguous end-to-end communications between two users.

Each device (such as a computer or workstation) on a communications link or network is identified with a physical address. This address is also called the hardware address. Many manufacturers place the physical address on a logic board within the device or in an interface unit connected directly to the device. Two physical addresses are employed in a communications dialogue; one address identifies the sender (source) and the other address identifies the receiver (destination). The length of the physical address varies, and most implementations use two 48-bit addresses.

The address detection operation on a LAN is illustrated in Figure A–1. Device A transmits a frame onto the channel. It is broadcast to all other stations attached to the channel, namely stations B, C, and D. We assume that the destination physical address (DPA) contains the value C. Consequently, stations B and D ignore the frame. Station C accepts it,

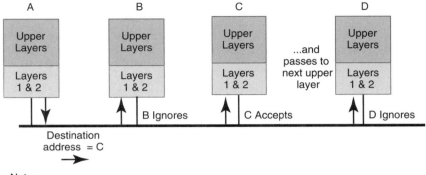

Figure A–1   Link address detection on a LAN.

performs several tasks associated with the physical layer, strips away the physical layer headers and trailers, and passes the remainder of the protocol data unit (PDU) (it is no longer called a frame) to the next upper layer.

The MAC Address

The IEEE assigns LAN addresses and universal protocol identifiers. Previously, this work was performed by the Xerox Corporation by administering what were known as block identifiers (Block IDs) for Ethernet addresses. The Xerox Ethernet Administration Office assigned these values, which were three octets (24 bits) in length. The organization that received this address was free to use the remaining 24 bits of the Ethernet address in any way it chose.

Due to the progress made in the IEEE 802 project, it was decided that the IEEE would assume the task of assigning these universal identifiers for all LANs, not just CSMA/CD types of networks. However, the IEEE continues to honor the assignments made by the Ethernet administration office, although it now calls the block ID an *organization unique identifier (OUI)*.

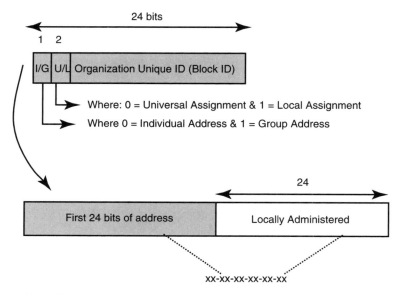

Figure A–2   The MAC address.

The format for the OUI is shown in Figure A–2. The least significant bit of the address space corresponds to the individual/group (I/G) address bit. The I/G address bit, if set to 0, means that the address field identifies an individual address. If the value is set to 1, the address field identifies a group address, which is used to identify more than one station connected to the LAN. If the entire OUI is set to all 1s, it signifies a broadcast address, which identifies all stations on the network.

The second bit of the address space is the local or universal bit (U/L). When this bit is set to 0, it has universal assignment significance—for example, from the IEEE. If it is set to 1, it is an address that is locally assigned. Bit position number two must always be set to 0, if it is administered by the IEEE.

The OUI is extended to include a 48-bit universal LAN address (which is designated as the *media access control [MAC]* address). The 24 bits of the address space is the same as the OUI assigned by the IEEE. The one exception is that the I/G bit may be set to 1 or 0 to identify group or individual addresses. The second part of the address space consisting of the remaining 24 bits is locally administered and can be set to any values an organization chooses.

The Network Address

A network address identifies a network, or networks. Part of the network address may also designate a computer, a terminal, or anything that a private network administrator wishes to identify within a network (or attached to a network), although the Internet standards place very strict rules on what an IP address identifies.

A network address is a higher level address than the physical address. The components in an internet that deal with network addresses need not be concerned with physical addresses until the data has arrived at the network link to which the physical device is attached.

This important concept is illustrated in Figure A–3. Assume that a user (host computer) in Los Angeles transmits packets to a packet network for relaying to a workstation on a LAN in London. The network in London has a network address of XYZ (this address scheme is explained shortly).

The packets are passed through the packet network (using the network's internal routing mechanisms) to the packet switch in New York. The packet switch in New York routes the packet to the gateway located in London. This gateway examines the destination network address in the packet and determines that the packet is to be routed to network

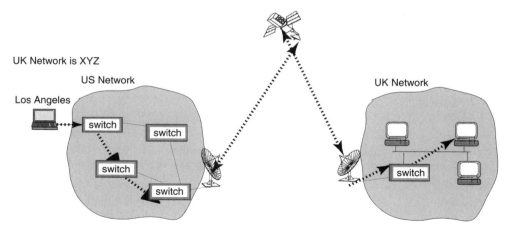

Figure A–3   Network layer addressing.

XYZ. It then transmits the packet onto the appropriate communications channel (link) to the node on the LAN that is responsible for communicating with the London gateway.

Notice that this operation did not use any physical addresses in these routing operations. The packet switches and gateway were only concerned with the destination network address of XYZ.

You might question how the London LAN is able to pass the packet to the correct device (host). As we learned earlier, a physical address is needed to prevent every packet from being processed by the upper layer network layer protocols residing in every host attached to the network. Therefore, the answer is that the target network (or gateway) must be able to translate a higher layer network destination address to a lower layer physical destination address.

Figure A–4, a node on the LAN, is a server that is tasked with address resolution. Let us assume that the destination address contains a network address, such as 128.1, *and* a host address, say 3.2. Therefore, the two addresses could be joined (concatenated) to create a full internet network address, which would appear as 128.1.3.2 in the destination address field of the IP datagram.

Once the LAN node receives the datagram from the gateway, it must examine the host address and either (a) perform a lookup into a table that contains the local physical address and its associated network address, or (b) query the station for its physical address. Then, it encapsulates the user data into the LAN frame, places the appropriate LAN

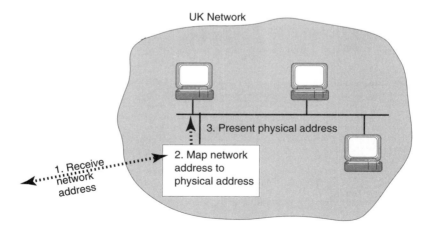

Figure A–4   Mapping network addresses to physical addresses.

physical layer address in the destination address of the frame, and transmits the frame onto the LAN channel. All devices on the network examine the physical address. If this address matches the device's address, the PDU is passed to the next upper layer; otherwise, it is ignored.

The IP Address

IP networks use a 32-bit, layer 3 address to identify a host computer and the network to which the host is attached. The structure of the IP address is depicted in Figure A–5. Its format is:

IP Address = Network Address + Host Address.

The IP address identifies a host's connection to its network. Consequently, if a host machine is moved to another network, its address must be changed.

IP addresses are classified by their formats. Four formats are permitted: class A, class B, class C, and class D formats. As illustrated in this figure, the first bits of the address specify the format of the remainder of the address field in relation to the network and host subfields. The host address is also called the local address (also called the REST field).

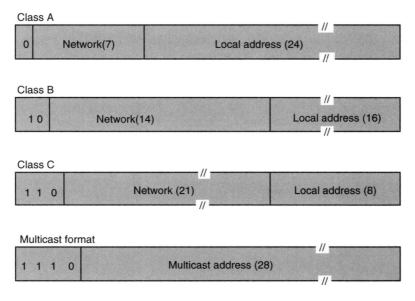

Figure A–5   Internet Protocol (IP) address formats.

The *class A* addresses provide for networks that have a large number of hosts. The host ID field is 24 bits. Therefore, 2^{24} hosts can be identified. Seven bits are devoted to the network ID, which supports an identification scheme for as many as 127 networks (bit values of 1 to 127).

Class B addresses are used for networks of intermediate size. Fourteen bits are assigned for the network ID, and 16 bits are assigned for the host ID. *Class C* networks contain fewer than 256 hosts (2^8). Twenty-one bits are assigned to the network ID. Finally, *class D* addresses are reserved for multicasting, which is a form of broadcasting, but within a limited area.

The IP address space can take the forms as shown in Table A–2, and the maximum network and host addresses that are available for the class A, B, and C addresses are also shown.

There are instances when an organization has no need to connect into the Internet or another private intranet. Therefore, it is not necessary to adhere to the IP addressing registration conventions, and the organization can use the addresses it chooses. It is important that it is certain that connections to other networks will not occur, since the use of addresses that are allocated elsewhere could create problems.

Table A-2   IP Addresses

	Network Address Space Values	
A	from: <u>0</u>.0.0.0	to: <u>127</u>.255.255.255*
B	from: <u>128</u> .0.0.0	to: <u>191</u>.255.255.255
C	from: <u>192</u>.0.0.0	to: <u>223</u>.255.255.255
D	from: <u>224</u>.0.0.0	to: <u>239</u>.255.255.255
E	from: <u>240</u>.0.0.0	to: <u>247</u>.255.255.255**

* Numbers 0 and 127 are reserved
** Reserved for future use

	Maximum Network Numbers	Maximum Host Numbers
A	126 *	16,777,124
B	16,384	65,534
C	2,097,152	254

* Numbers 0 and 127 are reserved

The addresses set aside for <u>private</u> allocations:

Class A addresses: 10.x.x.x – 10.x.x.x (1)

Class B addresses: 172.16.x.x – 172.31.x.x (16)

Class C addresses: 192.168.0.x – 192.168.255.x (256)

In RFC 1597, several IP addresses have been allocated for private addresses, and it is a good idea to use these addresses if an organization chooses not to register with the Internet. Systems are available that will translate private, unregistered addresses to public, registered addresses if connections to global systems are needed.

Figure A–6 shows examples of the assignment of IP address in more detail (examples use IP class B addresses). A common backbone (common net) connects three subnetworks: 176.16.2, 176.16.3, and 176.16.4. Routers act as the interworking units between the legacy (conventional) LANs and the backbone. The backbone could be a conventional Ethernet, but in most situations, the backbone is a Fiber Distributed Data Interface (FDDI), a Fast Ethernet node, or an ATM hub.

The routers are also configured as subnet nodes and access servers are installed in the network to support address and naming information services.

The IP datagram contains the source address and the destination address of the sender and receiver respectively. These two addresses do not change. They remain intact end-to-end. The destination address is used at each IP module to determine which "next node" is to receive the datagram. It is matched against the IP routing table to find the outgoing link to reach this next node.

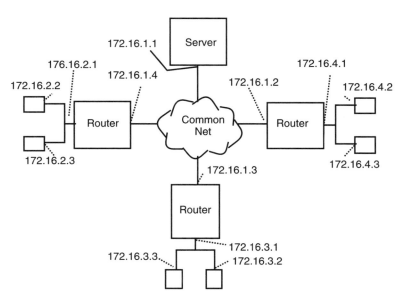

Figure A–6 Examples of IP addressing.

In contrast, the MAC source and destination addresses change as the frame is sent across each link. After all, MAC addresses have significance only at the link layer.

In Figure A–7, the IP source address of A.1 and destination address of C.2 stay the same throughout the journey through the Internet. The MAC addresses change at each link. It is necessary for the destination MAC address to contain the MAC address of the machine on the respective LAN that is to receive the frame. Otherwise, the frame cannot be delivered.

At first glance, it might appear that the IP addressing scheme is flexible enough to accommodate the identification of a sufficient number of networks and hosts to service almost any user or organization. But this is not the case. The Internet designers were not shortsighted; they simply failed to account for the explosive growth of the Internet as well as for the rapid growth of the IPs in private networks.

The problem arises when a network administrator attempts to identify a large number of networks and/or computers (such as personal computers) attached to these networks. The problem becomes onerous because of the need to store and maintain many network addresses and the associated requirement to access these addresses through large routing tables. The use of address advertising to exchange routing informa-

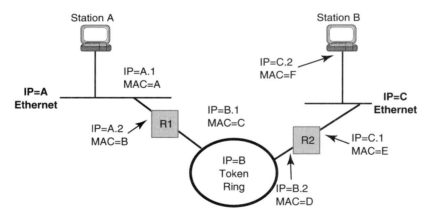

From	To	Source IP Address	Destination IP Address	Source MAC Address	Destination MAC Address
Station A	Router 1	A.1	C.2	A	B
Router 1	Router 2	A.1	C.2	C	D
Router 2	Station B	A.1	C.2	E	F

Figure A–7   Relationship of IP and MAC addresses.

tion requires immense resources if they must access and maintain big addressing tables.

The problem is compounded when networks are added to an internet. The addition requires the reorganization of routing tables and perhaps the assignment of additional addresses to identify the new networks.

To deal with this problem, the Internet establishes a scheme whereby multiple networks are identified by one address entry in the routing table. Obviously, this approach reduces the number of network addresses needed in an internet. It also requires a modification to the routing algorithms, but the change is minor in comparison to the benefits derived.

Figure A–8 shows the structure of the slightly modified internet address. All that has taken place is the division of the local address, heretofore called the host address, into the subnet address and the host address.

It is evident that both the initial Internet address and the subnet address take advantage of hierarchical addressing and hierarchical routing. This concept fits well with the basic gateway functions inherent in the Internet.

The choice of the assignments of the "local address" is left to the individual network implementors. There are many choices in the definition of the local address. As we mentioned before, it is a local matter, but it does require considerable thought. It requires following the same theme of the overall Internet address of how many subnets must be identified in relation to how many hosts that reside on each subnet must be identified.

In order to support subnet addressing, the IP routing algorithm is modified to support a subnet mask. The purpose of the mask is to determine which part of the IP address pertains to the subnetwork and which part pertains to the host.

The convention used for subnet masking is to use a 32-bit field in addition to the IP address. The contents of the field (the mask) are set as shown in Figure A–8.

Table A–3 is provided to aid in correlating the IP binary subnet mask to hexadecimal and decimal equivalents. The table is self-descriptive.

Table A–4 is based on a table that appears in Chris Lewis's book.[1] It should be helpful if you are trying to determine how many subnets and hosts can be derived from different combinations of subnet masks. The tables are for class B and class C networks. One rule should be remem-

---

[1]The table in Chris Lewis' book on the class C subnet mask is in error (Mr. Lewis leaves out one iteration of 255; see page 38). It is not a big deal and does not distract from the overall quality of the book.

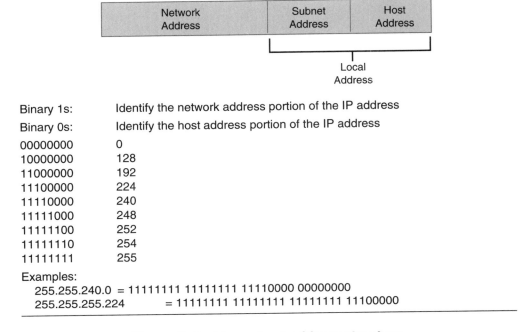

Binary 1s: Identify the network address portion of the IP address

Binary 0s: Identify the host address portion of the IP address

00000000   0
10000000   128
11000000   192
11100000   224
11110000   240
11111000   248
11111100   252
11111110   254
11111111   255

Examples:
    255.255.240.0 = 11111111 11111111 11110000 00000000
    255.255.255.224   = 11111111 11111111 11111111 11100000

Figure A–8   The subnet address structure.

bered: the first and last address of a host or subnet range of numbers cannot be used. They are reserved. So, if the range of the value is 3 bits (0 -7), the values permit 6 addresses. The first bit is used to identify the actual subnet number, and the last bit is used as the broadcast address for that subnet. Here is an example from the Chris Lewis reference.

        IP address   210.222.5.121
        Subnet mask   255.255.255.248

Table A–3 IP   Subnet Mask Values

Binary Values				Hex Values				Decimal Values			
1111 1111	1111 1111	1111 1111	1111 1111	FF	FF	FF	FF	255	255	255	255
1111 1111	1111 1111	1111 1111	1111 1110	FF	FF	FF	FE	255	255	255	254
1111 1111	1111 1111	1111 1111	1111 1100	FF	FF	FF	FC	255	255	255	252
1111 1111	1111 1111	1111 1111	1111 1000	FF	FF	FF	F8	255	255	255	248
1111 1111	1111 1111	1111 1111	1111 0000	FF	FF	FF	F0	255	255	255	240

Table A–3 IP (*continued*)

Binary Values				Hex Values				Decimal Values			
1111 1111	1111 1111	1111 1111	1110 0000	FF	FF	FF	E0	255	255	255	224
1111 1111	1111 1111	1111 1111	1100 0000	FF	FF	FF	C0	255	255	255	192
1111 1111	1111 1111	1111 1111	1000 0000	FF	FF	FF	80	255	255	255	128
1111 1111	1111 1111	1111 1111	0000 0000	FF	FF	FF	00	255	255	255	00
1111 1111	1111 1111	1111 1110	0000 0000	FF	FF	FE	00	255	255	254	00
1111 1111	1111 1111	1111 1100	0000 0000	FF	FF	FC	00	255	255	252	00
1111 1111	1111 1111	1111 1000	0000 0000	FF	FF	F8	00	255	255	248	00
1111 1111	1111 1111	1111 0000	0000 0000	FF	FF	F0	00	255	255	240	00
1111 1111	1111 1111	1110 0000	0000 0000	FF	FF	E0	00	255	255	224	00
1111 1111	1111 1111	1100 0000	0000 0000	FF	FF	C0	00	255	255	192	00
1111 1111	1111 1111	1000 0000	0000 0000	FF	FF	80	00	255	255	128	00
1111 1111	1111 1111	0000 0000	0000 0000	FF	FF	00	00	255	255	00	00
1111 1111	1111 1110	0000 0000	0000 0000	FF	FE	00	00	255	254	00	00
1111 1111	1111 1100	0000 0000	0000 0000	FF	FC	00	00	255	252	00	00
1111 1111	1111 1000	0000 0000	0000 0000	FF	F8	00	00	255	248	00	00
1111 1111	1111 0000	0000 0000	0000 0000	FF	F0	00	00	255	240	00	00
1111 1111	1110 0000	0000 0000	0000 0000	FF	E0	00	00	255	224	00	00
1111 1111	1100 0000	0000 0000	0000 0000	FF	C0	00	00	255	192	00	00
1111 1111	1000 0000	0000 0000	0000 0000	FF	80	00	00	255	128	00	00
1111 1111	0000 0000	0000 0000	0000 0000	FF	00	00	00	255	00	00	00
1111 1110	0000 0000	0000 0000	0000 0000	FE	00	00	00	254	00	00	00
1111 1100	0000 0000	0000 0000	0000 0000	FC	00	00	00	252	00	00	00
1111 1000	0000 0000	0000 0000	0000 0000	F8	00	00	00	248	00	00	00
1111 0000	0000 0000	0000 0000	0000 0000	F0	00	00	00	240	00	00	00
1110 0000	0000 0000	0000 0000	0000 0000	E0	00	00	00	224	00	00	00
1100 0000	0000 0000	0000 0000	0000 0000	C0	00	00	00	192	00	00	00
1000 0000	0000 0000	0000 0000	0000 0000	80	00	00	00	128	00	00	00
0000 0000	0000 0000	0000 0000	0000 0000	00	00	00	00	00	00	00	00

Table A–4   Class B and C Subnet Masks and Resultant Subnets and Hosts

Number of Bits	Subnet Mask	For Class B Resultant Subnets	Resultant Hosts
2	255.255.192.0	2	16392
3	255.255.224.0	6	8190
4	255.255.240.0	14	4094
5	255.255.248.0	30	2046
6	255.255.252.0	62	1022
7	255.255.254.0	126	510
8	255.255.225.0	254	254
9	255.255.225.128	510	126
10	255.255.225.192	1022	62
11	255.255.225.224	2046	30
12	255.255.225.240	4094	14
13	255.255.225.248	8190	6
14	255.255.225.252	16382	2

Number of Bits	Subnet Mask	For Class C Resultant Subnets	Resultant Hosts
2	255.255.225.192	2	62
3	255.255.225.224	6	30
4	255.255.225.240	14	14
5	255.255.225.248	30	6
6	255.255.225.252	62	2

Subnet address 201.222.5.120
Usable subnet host addresses 201.222.5.121 - 201.222.5.126
Subnet broadcast address   201.222.5.127

ADDRESS AGGREGATION AND SUBNET MASKS AND PREFIXES

Address aggregation is introduced in Chapter 1. It is the method used today to reduce the size of the routing tables. It is quite similar to the use of subnet masks, with the following exceptions: (a) the net and subnet bits are contiguous and begin in the high-order (most significant) part of the address space, (b) a 32-bit submask is not used, rather (c) a prefix value is appended to the end of an address to describe how many bits are to be used as the mask. In most routers, addresses can be configured with a conventional decimal notation, or a prefix.

Figure A–9 shows how address aggregation is used. The three subnets 172.16.1.0, 172.16.2.0, and 172.16.3.0 use a prefix of 24. This value means the net/subnet (actually, net/subnet lose their meaning now) span across the first 24 bits of the address, leaving the last 8 bits to identify the hosts.

However, router A does not have to advertise all three addresses. It aggregates these addresses into 172.16.0.0/16. The /16 means the first 16 bits of the advertised address pertains to networks (actually prefixes) at router A.

As a consequence of this approach, routers B and C do not have to store three addresses in their routing tables. They need only to store one address with its prefix. Whenever routers B and C receive an IP datagram with 172.16.x.x in the destination address, the use of a stored prefix value in the routing table enables the routers to know that the datagram is to be sent to router A.

Routers B and C are not concerned with knowing about any more details of the bit contents of the address beyond the prefix. It is router

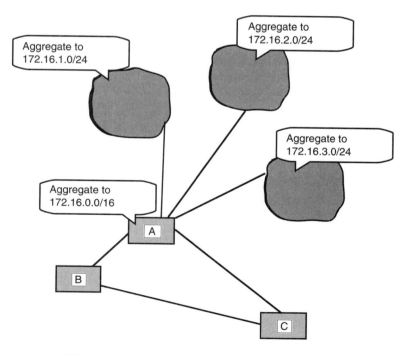

Figure A–9   Reducing routing table sizes.

A's job to know that the three networks are directly attached to router A's interfaces. Router A knows this fact because it has a special table containing the addresses of directly attached networks, and it consults this information before it accesses the long routing table.

Figure A–10 is a more detailed view of address aggregation. The arrows depict route advertising packets, more commonly known as routing packets. The small arrows are advertisements being sent from hosts and are conveyed to an assigned router on each of the three subnets. These routers are not shown in this figure. In this simple example, seven hosts are sending routing packets. Each subnet is aggregated with the prefix of 24, resulting in three packets being sent to router A.

Router A aggregates these advertisements to a prefix of 16 and sends routing packets to its neighbor routers, B and C.

These routers send this same advertisement to each other. Consequently, routers B and C know of two routes to 176.16.0/16. Under most

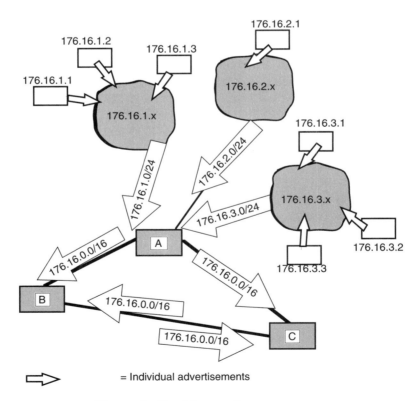

Figure A–10   The routing messages.

conditions, the most direct route would be chosen to these subnets; that is, directly through A. However, we will see that circumstances exist where B's packets to A might go through C first, and C's packets to A might go through B first. The obvious circumstance is a link failure between A and either B or C, but other circumstances are possible and are explained later.

One other situation needs explaining in this example. Routers A, B, and C are connected together in a loop. It is therefore conceptually possible for the routing packets to loop around over and over. Of course, measures are taken to preclude the looping of advertisements, and are also explained later.

Figure A–11 shows how a subnet mask is interpreted. Assume a class B IP address of 128.1.17.1, with a mask of 255.255.240.0. At a router, to discover the subnet address value, the mask has a bitwise Boolean *and* operation performed on the address, as shown in the figure (this address is in a routing table). The mask is also applied to the destination address in the datagram.

By the notation "don't care," it means that the router is not concerned at this point with the host address. It is concerned with getting the datagram to the proper subnetwork. So, in this example, it uses the mask to discover that the first 4 bits of the host address are to be used for the subnet address. Further, it discovers that the subnet address is 1.

As this example shows, when the subnet mask is split across octets, the results can be a bit confusing if you are "octet-aligned." In this case, the actual value for the subnet address is 0001_2 or 1_{10}, even though the decimal address of the host space is 17.1. However, the software does not

	128.	1.	17.	1
IP address	10000000	00000001	0001|0001	00000001
Mask	11111111	11111111	1111|0000	00000000
Result	10000000	00000001	0001|	don't care
Logical address	128	1	1|	don't care
		network	sub net|	host

Note: "don't care" means router doesn't care at this time
(the router is looking for subnet matches)

Figure A–11   Example of address masking operations.

care about octet alignment. It is looking for a match of the destination address in the IP datagram to an address in a routing table, based on the mask that is stored in the routing table.

The class address scheme (A, B, C) has proved to be too inflexible to meet the needs of the growing Internet. For example, the class address of 47 means that three bytes are allocated to identify hosts attached to network 47, resulting in 2^{24} hosts on the single network—clearly not realistic! Moreover, the network.host address does not allow more than a two-level hierarchical view of the address. Multiple levels of hierarchy are preferable, because it permits using fewer entries in routing tables and the aggregation of lower-level addresses to a higher-level address.

The introduction of subnets in the IP address opened the way to better utilize the IP address space by implementing a multilevel-level hierarchy. This approach allows the aggregation of networks to reduce the size of routing tables.

Figure A–12 is derived [HALA 98][2] and shows the advertising operations that occur without route aggregation (without Classless Interdomain Routing (CIDR), discussed next). The ISPs are ultimately advertising all their addresses to the Internet to a network access point (NAP). Four addresses are shown here, but in an actual situation, thousands of addresses might be advertised.

In contrast to the above example, where each address is advertised to the Internet, the use of masks allows fewer addresses to be advertised. In Figure A–13, ISP1 and ISP2 are using masks of 16 bits in length (255.255.0.0), and ISP1 need only advertise address 192.168.0.0 with the 16-bit mask to inform all interested nodes that all addresses behind this mask can be found at 192.168.x.x. ISP1 uses the same mask to achieve the same goal.

ISP3 uses a mask of 8 bits (255.0.0.0), which effectively aggregates the addresses of ISP1 and ISP2 under the aggregation domain of ISP3. Thus, in this simple example, one address instead of four is advertised to the NAP.

In order to extend the limited address space of an IP address, CIDR is now used in many systems and is required for operations between autonomous systems. It permits networks to be grouped together logically and to use one entry in a routing table for multiple class C networks.

This example shows how the concept works. The first requirement for CIDR is for multiple networks to share a certain number of bits in the high-order part of the IP address. In this example, the first 7 bits in the address are the same. Thus, by using the mask of 254.0.0.0

[2][HALA 98] Halabi, Bassam, "Internet Routing Architectures," Cisco Press, 1998.

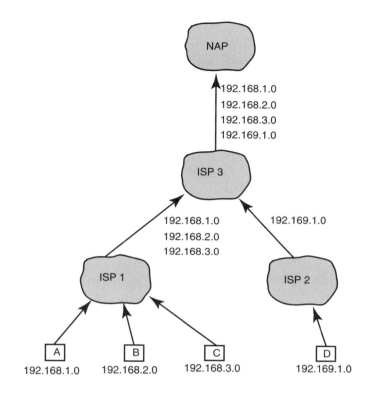

Where:
  NAP: Network access point
  ISP: Internet service provider

Figure A–12   Without aggregation.

(11111110.00000000.00000000.00000000), all addresses between 194.0.0.0 and 195.255.255.255 can be identified by a single entry in the routing table.

Once the point in the network has been reached, the remainder of the address space can be used for hierarchical routing. For example, a mask of say 255.255.240.0 could be used to group networks together. This concept, if carried out on all IP addresses (and not just class C addresses), would result in the reduction of an Internet routing table from about 10,000 entries to 200 entries.

Additional information on CIDR is available in RFCs 1518, 1519, 1466, and 1447, and summarized in Table A–5.

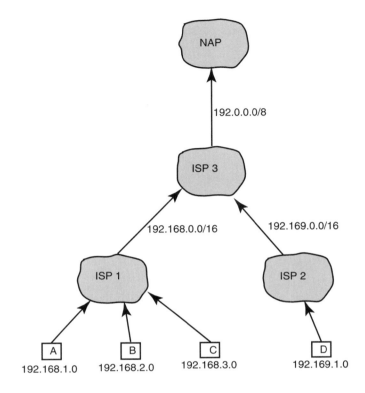

Note: The notations /16 and /8 refer to the lengths of masks.

Where:
NAP: Network access point
ISP: Internet service provider

Figure A–13   With aggregation.

VARIABLE LENGTH SUBMASKS

Subnet masks are useful in internetworking operations, especially the variable length subnet mask. This figure (which is a summary of a more detailed example from the Halabi reference) shows the idea of VLSM.

We assume an organization is using a class C address of 192.168.1.x. The organization needs to set up three networks (subnets) as shown in Figure A–14. Subnet A has 100 hosts attached to it, and subnets B and C support 50 hosts each.

Table A–5   Classless Interdomain Routing (CIDR) ("Supernetting")

- Reduces the size of routing tables
- Requirements:
  - Multiple IP addresses must share a specific number of high-order bits of an address
  - Masks must be used
  - Routing protocols must support the masks
- Example (from RFC 1466):
  - Addresses from 194.0.0.0 through 195.255.255.255
  - 65536 different class C addresses, but the first 7 bits are the same: 1100001x (they show the same high-order 7 bits)
  - One entry in a routing table of 194.0.0.0 with a mask of 254.0.0.0 suffices of all addresses (to a single point)
- A longer mask can be used to route to addresses beyond first mask

Recall from our previous discussions that the subnet mask is used to determine how many bits are set aside for the subnet and host addresses. This figure shows the possibilities for the class C address. (The resultant numbers in the table assume that the IP address reserved numbers are used, which is possible, since 192.168.1.x is from a pool of private addresses and can be used as the organization chooses.)

The use of one mask for the three subnets will not work. A mask of 255.255.255.128 yields only 2 subnets, and a mask of 255.255.255.192 yields only 64 hosts.

Fortunately, different subnetwork masks can be used on each subnet. As the figure shows, subnet A uses subnet mask 255.255.255.128, and subnets B and C use subnet mask 255.255.255.192.

Not all route discovery protocols support subnetwork masks. So, check your product before you delve into this operation.

THE HIGH OVERHEAD OF IP FORWARDING

With the advent of subnet operations, the routing operations to support diverse topology and addressing needs are greatly enhanced. As an added bonus, the 32-bit IP address space is utilized more effectively.

However, these features translate into a more complex set of operations at the router. Moreover, as the Internet and internets continue to grow, the router may be required to maintain large routing tables. In a conventional routing operation, summarized in this figure, the process-

Class C Address of 192.168.1.x is used by an organization

Organization needs the following topology:

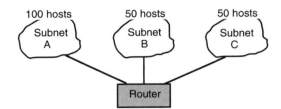

Possible Masks:

Subnet Mask	Resultant Subnets*	Resultant Hosts*
255.255.255.128	2	128
255.255.255.192	4	64
255.255.255.224	8	32
255.255.255.240	16	16
255.255.255.248	32	8
255.255.255.252	64	4

* Assumes use of reserved bits

Use .128 yields 2 subnets with 128 hosts each: Won't work

Use .192 yields 4 subnets with 64 hosts each: Won't work

Answer? Use both (Variable length subnet mask):

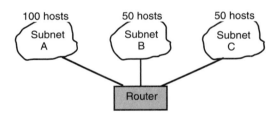

Subnet A mask = 255.255.255.128
Subnet B mask = 255.255.255.192
Subnet C mask = 255.255.255.192

Figure A–14   Managing the IP addresses.

ing load to handle many addresses in combination with subnet operations can lead to serious utilization problems for the router.

Part of the overhead stems from the fact that a network can be configured with different subnet masks. The router must check each entry in the routing table to ascertain the mask, even though the table addresses may point to the same network. This concept is called a variable length submask (VLSM), and provides a lot of flexibility in configuring different numbers of hosts to different numbers of subnets. For example, a class C address could use different subnet masks to identify different numbers of hosts attached to different subnets in an enterprise, say 120 hosts at one site, and 62 at another.

To route traffic efficiently, the router must prune (eliminate) table entries that do not match the masked portion of the table entry and the destination IP address in the datagram. After the table is pruned, the remaining entries must be searched for the longest match, and "more general" route masks are discarded.

After all these operations, the router has to deal with the type of service (in practice, TOS may not be implemented), the best metric, and perhaps special procedures dealing with routing policies.

For high-end routers that are placed in the Internet to interwork between the large Internet service providers, the routing table could contain several thousand entries. To execute the operations of masking, table pruning, and longest mask matching requires extensive computational resources.

Because of this overhead, the high-end routers are taking a different approach, called IP label switching, the topic of this book.

Appendix B:

CR-LDP and Traffic Engineering and QOS

In chapters 5, 6, 7, and 9 the subjects of traffic engineering (TE) and quality of service (QOS) are explained in relation to MPLS. In several of these explanations, constraint-based routing with LDP (CR-LDP) was also included. As a follow up to these discussions, this appendix provides more details on how CR-LDP interworks with DiffServ, ATM, RSVP, and Frame Relay to support the customer's QOS requirements. The tables in this appendix are sourced from a white paper by Nortel Networks, and I wish to thank Nortel Networks[1] for their contributions to my work on computer networks.

In order to understand the material in this appendix you should be familiar with material in the chapters cited above.

The tables in this appendix contain entries called "local behavior." This term refers to the operations of the network nodes (typically label switching routes) in how they handle packet forwarding functions.

---

[1]Using CR-LDP for Service Interworking, Traffic Engineering, and Quality of Service in Carrier Networks. Document number 55049.25/09-00. Go to www.nortelnetworks.com or contact Marketing Publications, Dept. 9244, PO Box 13010, RTP NC 27709.

CR-LDP AND ATM QOS

In chapter 6, it is emphasized that MPLS must be able to interwork with ATM, since ATM is a prevalent technology in wide area and metropolitan networks. In chapter 9, several examples are provided of the LDP message parameters, some of which are closely associated with ATM service categories. Table B–1 provides more details on these relationships.

For the ATM conformance definitions, the ITU-T and ATM Forum Generic Cell Rate Algorithm (GRCA) is used and is explained in chapter 7. Many of the parameters listed in this table have been explained throughout this book, but is should prove helpful to describe them in one place, and offer explanations on the ATM parameters (they are described in more detail in the ATM books in this series).

Parameters for ATM/CR-LDP Interworking

The Peak Cell Rate Reference Model.   The ATM Forum specifications provide a reference model to describe the peak cell rate (PCR). This model is shown in Figure B–1. It consists of an equivalent terminal, which contains the traffic sources, a multiplexer (MUX), and a virtual shaper. The term equivalent terminal means a model of a user device that performs the functions described in this discussion.

The traffic sources offer cells to a multiplexer (MUX), with each source offering cells at its own rate. Typically, the cells are offered from the AAL through the service access point (SAP). The MUX then offers all these cells to the virtual shaper. The job of the virtual shaper is to smooth the cell flow that is offered to the physical layer and the ATM UNI (private UNI).

The GCRA comes into play in this model at three interfaces: (a) at the boundary between the ATM layer and the physical layer (the PhSAP, for physical service access point), (b) at the private user network interface (UNI), and (c) at the public UNI.

For this discussion, we define T as the peak emission interval of the connection, and the minimal inter-arrival time between two consecutive cells is greater than or equal to T. The PCR of the ATM connection is the inverse of the minimum arrival time between two cells.

The output of the virtual shaper at the PhSAP conforms to GCRA (T,0). The output at the private UNI and public UNI is different because cell delay variation (CDV) will exist in the physical layer of the equivalent terminal (user device) and the node between this device and the network. Therefore, the private UNI conforms to GRCA (T,t^*) and the public

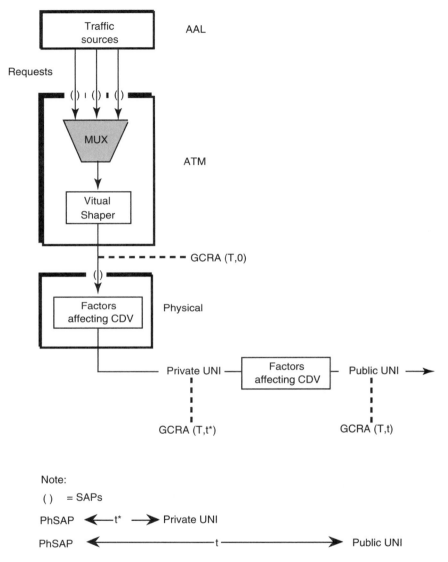

Figure B–1   Reference model for peak cell rate (PCR)

UNI conforms to GRCA (T,t), where t is the cell delay tolerance. The latter value takes into consideration the additional CDV between the PhSAP and the public UNI.

The ATM network does not set the peak emission interval T at the user device. T can be set to account for different profiles of traffic, as long as the MUX buffers remain stable. Thus, T's reciprocal can be any value that is greater than the sustainable rate, but (of course) not greater than the link rate.

Cell Delay Variation Tolerance (CDVT). A certain amount of delay is encountered when cells are vying for the same output port of the multiplexer, or when signaling cells inserted in to the stream. As a result, with the reference to the peak emission interval T (which is the inverse of PCR R_p), randomness is instilled in the inter-arrival time between consecutive cells.

The 1-point CDV for cell $k(y_k)$ at the measurement point is the difference between the cell's reference arrival time (c_k), and the actual arrival time (a_k) at the measurement point: $y_k = c_k - a_k$. The reference arrival time (c_k) is:

$$c_0 = a_0 = {}_0$$

$$c_k + 1 = \begin{cases} c_k + T \text{ if } c_k \geq a_k \text{ otherwise} \\ a_k + T \end{cases}$$

The 2-point CDV or cell $k(v_k)$ between two measurement points MP_1 and MP_2 is the difference between the absolute cell transfer delay of cell $k(x_k)$ between the two MPs and a defined reference cell transfer delay $(d_{1,2})$ between MP1 and MP2: $v_k = v_k - d_{1,2}$.

The absolute cell transfer delay (xk) of cell k between MP_1 and MP_2 is the same as the cell transfer delay defined earlier. The reference cell transfer delay (d1,2) between MP_1 and MP_2 is the absolute cell transfer delay experienced by a reference cell between the two MPs.

The CR-LDP Parameters.

This part of the appendix reviews the CR-LDP parameters that were explained in several parts of this book.

- Peak data rate (PDR): The maximum rate at which the traffic can be sent to the CR-label switched path (CR-LSP). It is defined with a token bucket with the parameters peak data rate (PDR) and peak burst size (PBS).
- Peak Burst Size (PBS): The maximum burst size allowed at the peak data rate (PDR).
- Committed Data Rate (CDR): The rate that the MPLS domain commits for the CR-LSP. It is defined with the parameters committed data rate (CDR), and committed burst rate (CBR).

- Committed burst size (CBS): The maximum burst size allowed at the committed data rate (CDR). When the CBS bucket is full, it overflows into the excess burst rate (EBS) bucket.
- Excess burst size (EBS): Measures the extent to which traffic sent on the path exceeds the committed data rate (CDR). It is defined as an additional limit on the CDR/s token bucket.

CR-LDP Interworking with ATM QOS

Table B–1 shows the relationships of CR-LDP and ATM QOS. The label switching router (LSR) at the edge of the network is expected to enforce these parameters: (a) PDR, (b) PBS, (c) CDR, and (d) CBS.

CR-LDP AND FRAME RELAY QOS

Table B–2 shows the relationships of CR-LDP and Frame Relay services. Recall that Frame Relay basic operations are explained in chapter 6. The Frame Relay service categories and parameters are explained as notes to Table B–2.

CR-LDP AND RSVP TRAFFIC ENGINEERING (RSVP-TE)

We learned in Chapter 5 that the Resource Reservation Protocol (RSVP) is used to reserve resources for a session in an Internet. RSVP can provide guaranteed service (GS) by reserving the necessary resources at each machine that participates in supporting the flow of traffic, as established in RFC 2212. Although not discussed in chapter 5, RSVP also is defined to support a controlled load service (CLS), defined in RFC 2211. Table B–3 shows the relationships of CR-LDP and RSVP-TE.

Table B–1 Cross-Referencing of ATM Service Categories to CR-LDP QOS Parameters

ATM Service Categories		CR-LDP QoS Parameters		
ATM Services	ATM Conference Definition	Parameter Mapping	Edge Rules	Local Behavior
CBR	GCRA1(T0 + 1, CDVT)	PDR = 1/T0 + 1 PBS → CDVT	Drop packets > (PDR, PBS)	Very Frequent
VBR.1	GCRA1(T0 + 1 CDVT) GCRA2(Ts0 + 1 + BT 0 + 1 + CDVT)	PDR = 1/T0 + 1 PBS → CDVT CDR = 1/Ts0 + 1 CBS → BT0 + 1 + CDVT	Drop packets > (PDR, PBS) Drop packets > (CDR, CBS)	Frequent or Unspecified
VBR.2	GCRA1(T0 + 1, CDVT) GCRA2(Ts0 + BT0 + CDVT)	PDR = 1/T0 + 1 PBS → CDVT CDR = 1/Ts0 CBS → BT0 + CDVT	Drop packets > (PDR, PBS) Drop packets > (CDR, CBS)	Frequent or Unspecified
VBR.3	GCRA1(T0 + 1, CDVT) GCRA2(Ts0 + BT0 + CDVT)	PDR = 1/T0 + 1 PBS → CDVT CDR = 1/Ts0 CBS → BT0 + CDVT	Drop packets > (PDR, PBS) Tag packets > (CDR, CBS)	Frequent or Unspecified
UBR.1	GCRA(T0 + 1, CDVT)	PDR = 1/T0 + 1) PBS → CDVT	Network specific; (Tagging is not allowed.)	Unspecified
UBR.2	GCRA(T0 + 1, CDVT)	PDR = 1/T0 + 1 PBS → CDVT	Network specific; (Tagging is not allowed.)	Unspecified

Notes to Table B–1:

• The Frequency parameter — Frequent or Unspecified — for VBR services depends on whether or not the service is real-time.
• The mapping between the Cell Delay Variation Tolerance (CDVT) and the Peak Burst Size (PBS) and the Burst Tolerance (BT) and the Committed Data Size (CDS) is as specified in the ATM Forum standards.

Table B–2 Cross Referencing of Frame Relay Services to CR-LDP QOS Parameters

| ATM Service Categories | | CR-LDP QOS Parameters | | |
Service	Parameters	Parameter Mapping	Edge Rules	Local Behavior
Default	AR, CIR, Bc, Be	PDR = AR CDR = CIR CBS = Bc EBS = Be	Police PDR, CDR, CBS, and EBS Drop Packets > PDR or > Be Tag packets > Bc but within Be	Unspecified
Mandatory	AR, CIR, Bc, Be	PDR = AR CDR = CIR CBS = Bc EBS = Be	Police PDR, CDR, CBS, and EBS Drop Packets > PDR or > Be Tag packet > Bc but within Be	Unspecified
Optional1	AR, CIR, Bc, Be	PDR = AR CDR = CIR CBS = Bc EBS = Be	Police PDR, CDR, CBS, and EBS Drop Packets > PDR or > Be Tag packet > Bc but within Be	Very Frequent
Optional2	AR, CIR, Bc, Be	PDR = AR CDR = CIR CBS = Bc EBS = Be	Police PDR, CDR, CBS, and EBS Drop Packets > PDR or > Be Tag packet > Bc but within Be	Frequent

Notes to Table B–2:

- Committed Rare Measurement Interval (Tc) — The time interval during which the user is allowed to send only the committed amount of data (Bc) and the excess amount of data (Bc). Tc is computed at Bc/CIR.
- Committed Information Rate (CIR) — The information transfer rate at which the network is committed to transfer under normal conditions. The rate is averaged over a minimum increment of time Tc. CIR is negotiated at call setup.
- Committed Burst Size (Bc) — The maximum committed amount of data a user may offer to the network during a time interval Tc. Bc is negotiated at call setup.
- Excess Burst Size (Be) — The maximum allowed amount of data by which a user can exceed Bc during a time interval Tc. Be is delivered, in general, with a lower than Bc. Be is negotiated at call setup.
- Access Rate (AR) — *Data rate of the user access channel.*

Table B-3 Cross-Referencing of RSVP-TE Services to CR-LDP QOS Parameters

RSVP-TE Service			CR-LDP QOS Parameters		
Service	Service Parameters	Parameter Mapping	Edge Rules		Local Behavior
GS	p, b, r, m, and M	PDR = p CDR = r CBS = b	• At any interval of length T, traffic should not exceed ([M + min[pT, rT, + b − M]). • Non-conforming packets are treated as best effort.		Very Frequent
CLS	b, r, m, and M p is optional	PDR = p CDR = r CBS = b	• At any interval of length T, traffic should not exceed [rT + b]. • Non-conforming packets are treated as best effort.		Frequent

Notes to Table B-3:

Similarities Between GS and CLS

- Both are real-time services that must be "hardwired" by correlating the edge rules to the local behavior. The main difference between the two services is the nature of the delay guarantee.
- Both services are defined at the network edge by the following token bucket parameters, which are collectively called Tspec parameters:
  - p = Peak rate of the flow (optional for CLS)
  - b = Bucket depth
  - t = Token bucket rate
  - m = Minimum policed unit
  - M = Maximum policed unit
- Traffic is policed at the edge, and the usual enforcing policy is to forward non-conforming packets as best effort.

Differences Between GS and CLS

- GS provides a hard mathematical upper boundary of packet delays, and CLS provides a delay that is equivalent to that seen by a best-effort service on a lightly loaded network.
- GS requires the reshaping of traffic to the token bucket parameters to meet the service delay requirements.
- GS also has Rspec parameters for the level of reservation in the RSVP domain, but because the RSVP terminates at the IWU and on Inter-working Unit, these parameters are not extended to the CR-LDP region.

Glossary

AAL	ATM adaptation layer	DLCI	data link connection ID
ABR	available bit rate	DNS	Domain Name System
ACK	Acknowledgment	DPA	destination physical address
AF	assured forwarding	DS	Differentiated Services
ASIC	application-specific integrated circuits	DSCP	DS codepoint
		EBS	excess burst size
ATM	Asynchronous Transfer Mode	EF	expedited forwarding
BA	behavior aggregate	E-LSP	EXP-inferred PSC LSP
BECN	backward explicit congestion notification	ER	explicit routing
		ERO	explicit route object
BGP	Border Gateway Protocol	EWMA	exponential weighted moving average
BL	burst limit		
BT	burst tolerance	EXP/LU	experimental/local use
BTT	bidirectional traffic trunk	FCS	frame check sequence
C/R	command response	FDDI	Fiber Distributed Data Interface
CBR	constant bit rate		
CBS	committed burst size	FEC	functional equivalence class
CDR	committed data rate	FECN	forward explicit congestion notification
CIDR	Classless Interdomain Routing		
CLP	cell loss priority	FIFO	first-in, first-out
CoS	cost of service	FMP	Flow Management Protocol
CQ	custom queuing	FTN	FEC-to-NHLFE
CR	constraint-based routing	GC/PRA	Generic Cell/Packet Rate Algorithm
CR	committed rate		
CR-LDP	Constraint-Based LDP	GFC	generic flow control
CU	currently unused	GPRA	generic packet rate algorithm
DE	discard eligibility	GR	guaranteed rate

223

GSMP	General Switch Management Protocol	PQ	priority queuing
		PSB	PHB scheduling class
HDLC	high-level data link control	PTI	payload type identifier
HEC	header error control	PVC	permanent virtual circuit
I/G	individual/group	QOS	quality of service
ICMP	Internet Control Message Protocol	RESV	Reservation
		RSVP	Resource Reservation protocol
IETF	Internet Engineering Taskforce	RTT	round-trip time
IGMP	Internet Group Message Protocol	SAFI	Subsequent Address Family Identifier
IGP	Internal Gateway Protocol	SAR	segmentation and reassembly
ILM	Incoming Label Map	SLA	service level agreement
ISP	Internet service provider	SR	service representation
LAN	local area network	STDM	statistical time division multiplexing
LB	local binding		
LCN	logical channel number	SVC	switched virtual circuit
LCT	last conformance time	TAT	theoretical arrival time
LDP	Label Distribution Protocol	TB	token bucket
L-LSP	lable-only-inferred PSC LSP	TCB	traffic conditioning block
LSP	label switched path	TCP	Transmission Control Protocol
LSR	label switching router	TDM	time division multiplexing
MAC	Media Access Control	TDP	Tag Distribution Protocol
MF	multifield	TE	traffic engineering
MGR	multigigabyte router	TFIB	tag forwarding information base
MPC	MPOA client		
MPLS	Multiprotocol Label Switching	TIB	tag information base
MPOA	Multiprotocol Over ATM	TLV	type-length-value
MPS	MPOA server	TOS	type of service
NAP	network access point	TP	traffic profile
NHLFE	Next Hop Label Forwarding Entry	TSR	tag switching router
		TTL	time to live
NHRP	Next Hop Resolution Protocol	UDP	User Data Protocol
NNI	network-node interface	UNI	user-to-network interface
NSAP	Network Service Access Point	UPC	usage parameter control
OA	ordered aggregate	VBR	variable bit rate
OAM	operations, administration, and maintenance	VC	virtual circuit
		VCC	virtual channel connection
OSI	Open Systems Interconnection	VCI	virtual channel identifier
OSPF	Open Shortest Path First	VCID	virtual circuit ID
OUI	organization unique identifier	VLSM	variable length subnet mask
PDU	protocol data unit	VPC	virtual path connection
PDV	packet delay variation	VPI	virtual path identifier
PHB	per-hop behavior	VPI/VCI	Virtual Path ID/Virtual Channel ID
PID	Protocol ID		
PPS	packets per second	WFQ	weighted fair queuing

References

[ANDE00] Anderson, Loa, et. al., "LDP Specification," *draft-ietf-mpls-ldp-11.txt,* August, 2000.

[ANDE99] Anderson, Loa, et. al., "MPLS Capability Set," *draft-loa-mpls-cap-set-01.txt,* October, 1999.

[AWDU00] Awduche, Daniel, O., et. al., "RSVP-TE: Extensions to RSVP for LSP Tunnels," *draft-ietf-mpls-rsvp-lsp-tunnel-05.txt,* February, 2000.

[AWDU99] Awduche, W., et. al., "Requirements for Traffic Engineering Over MPLS," RFC 2702, September 1999.

[BERN99] Bernet, Y., et al., "A Conceptual Model for DiffServ Routers," *draft-ietf-fid-dserv-model-00.txt,* June, 1999.

[BONI99] Bonica, R., et. al., "ICMP Extensions for MultiProtocol Label Switching," *draft-ietf-mpls-icmp-01.txt,* December, 1999.

[CONT98] Conta, A, et. al., "Use of Label Switching on Frame Relay Networks," *draft-ietf-mpls-fr-03.txt,* November, 1998.

[DAVI00] Davie, Bruce and Rekhter, Yakov, *MPLS: Technology and Applications,* San Diego: Academic Press, 2000.

[DAVI99], Davie, Bruce, et. al., "MPLS Using LDP and ATMVC Switching," *draft-ietf-mple-amt-02.txt.* April, 1999

[FAUC00] Le Faucheur, Francois, et al., "MPLS Support of Differentiated Services," *draft-ietf-mpls-diff-ext-04.txt,* March, 2000.

[FORO00] MPLS Forum 2000 Conference, 7–10 March, 2000, Hotel Sofitel, Rive Gauche, France.

[HALA98] Halabi, Bassam, "Internet Routing Achitectures," Cisco Press, 1998.

[HEIN99] Heinanen, J., et al., "Assured Forwarding PHB Group," RFC 2597, June, 1999.

[HEIN99] Heinanen, J., et al., RFC 2597, "Assured Forwarding PHB Group," June, 1999.

[JACO99] Jacobson, V., et al. , RFC 2598,"An Expedited Forwarding PHB," June 1999.

[JAMOO00] Jamoussi, Bilel. "Constrain-Based LSP Setup Using LDP," *draft-ietf-mpls-cr-ldp-03.txt,* September 1999.

[JAMO99] Jamoussi, Belel, et. al., "Constraint-Based LSP Setup Using LDP," *draft-ietf-mpla-cr-ldp-03.txt,* September, 1999.

[LIWE00] Liwen, Wu., et al., "MPLS Support of Differentiated Servies," *draft-ietf-mple-diff-ext-04.txt,* March 2000.

[NAGA00], Nagami, Ken-ichi, et. al., "VCID Notification over ATM for LDP," *draft-ietf-mpla-vcid-atm-o4.txt,* July, 1999.

[REKT00] Rekhter, Yakov and Rosen, Eric C., "Carrying Label Information in BGP-4." *draft-ietf-mpls-bgp4–04.txt,* January 2000.

[ROSE00] Rosen, Eric C. et al., "Multiprotocol Label Switching Architecture," *draft-ietf-mpls-07.txt*, July 2000.

[ROSE99a] Rosen, Eric C., "MPLS Label Stack Encoding," *draft-ietf-mpls-label-encaps-07.txt*, September, 1999.

[WENT97] Wentworth, R., ATM Forum Contribution 97–0980, December 1997.

[WIDJ99], Widjaja, I., and Elwalid A., "Performance Issues in VC-Merge Capable ATM LSRs," RFC 2682, September, 1999.

[WORS98] Worster, Tom, Wentworth, Robert. "Guaranteed Rate in Differentiated Services," *draft-worster-diffserv-gr-00.txt,* June 1998.

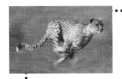

Index